Ambition
English Communication I
Workbook

解答・解説

開隆堂

Lesson 1

(pp.4-11)

For Better Communication

Part 1 基本問題

1 (1) at (2) returning (3) would

  (4) shocked (5) to

2 (1) a series of (2) lecture

  (3) viewpoint (4) distributed

3 (1) conservative to a certain degree

  (2) the use of talking to him

  (3) His duty as the principal of the school

  (4) your boss ought to scold you

4 (1)(例) The movie was so boring.

  (2)(例) He studies at home after school.

  (3)(例) I went to a café to talk with my
     friend(s).

  (4)(例) My mother likes writing letters.
     (例) My mother likes to write letters.

Part 2 基本問題

1 (1) down (2) paper (3) in

  (4) give (5) excited

2 (1) afford (2) income

  (3) disadvantage (4) heading

3 (1) Ms. Tanaka taught us English

  (2) free to rent for the musical

  (3) do yesterday instead of going to school

  (4) may lose a good chance to make some
     money

4 (1)(例) In fact, Miki and I were at home at
     that time.

  (2)(例) This project has a lot of advantages.
     (例) There are a lot of advantages of this
     project.

  (3)(例) He said that he would not[wouldn't]
     go there the next day.

  (4)(例) Increasing your income is not so
     (that) easy.

     (例) It is not so(that) easy to increase
     your income.

Part 3 基本問題

1 (1) advertising (2) is worth

  (3) the other (4) carefully

  (5) making

2 (1) Mind (2) review

  (3) reduction (4) would

3 (1) He gave me his final decision

  (2) handed the sheet of paper to the student

  (3) of the show is as well-known as its actors

  (4) Those lectures attract crowds of intelligent
     people to

4 (1)(例) I received it and replied to him the
     next day.

  (2)(例) The Internet has a lot of advantages
     and disadvantages.

  (3)(例) We talked about the way to get to
     the station.

  (4)(例) The company started[began]
     advertising in the newspaper(s).

     (例) The company started[began] to
     advertise in the newspaper(s).

Part 4 基本問題

1 (1) raising (2) in (3) At

  (4) well (5) down

2 (1) ridiculous (2) obvious

  (3) if (4) argument

3 (1) ought to talk with your parents about it
     [talk about it with your parents]

  (2) We all have an ability to connect with

  (3) your point of view on online education

(4) important to see things from the other person's angle

4 (1)(例)This coffee is too hot to drink.

(2)(例)She gave me some good advice.

(3)(例)They studied very[so] hard to pass the exam.

(4)(例)He thought that 90% of the people on the earth would ignore it.

Grammar　練習問題

1 (1) ②　(2) ④　(3) ②　(4) ①　(5) ③

2 (1) feel cold 　　　　(2) gets angry

(3) keep us 　　　　(4) busy preparing

(5) to eat 　　　　　(6) could

(7) stopped raining 　(8) only to

(9) before having[eating]

3 (1) The news that all members of the group were safe made us happy

(2) is to introduce many unknown cultures

(3) our English teacher taught us how to use a dictionary

(4) I will get you the ticket

(5) was relieved to hear my son could arrive there

(6) Japanese people are not good at expressing their opinions

(7) It's fun for me to see my pet cat's reaction

4 (1)(例)She succeeded in getting

(2)(例)She found the book very boring.

(3)(例)My brother became a lawyer

(4)(例)Eating too much (has) made me sleepy.

(5)(例)She said (that) she would never

(6)(例)I want[would like] to do my best

(7)(例)have a lot of homework to do

(8)(例)A bus will not come

(9)(例)Would you mind my[me] sitting

(10)(例)My dream is returning to

発展問題

(1) 自分で外国に行って（足を踏み入れて），文化の違いに気づくこと。

(2) 1つの国に長くいるほど，（その国の）人々がどのように意思疎通を図るかなど，より微妙な違いに多く気づくだろう。

(3) close, far, culture

(4) イ　　(5) ウ

＜全訳＞

　　より深いコミュニケーションの理解

　外国を訪れることで，①その国の文化をじかに経験できる。本を読んだり，インターネットの動画を見たりして文化を学ぶことができるが，ある国に足を踏み入れ，自身で文化の違いに気づく方がずっと興味深い。もちろん，最も明らかに違うことは言語，食べ物，服の着方などかもしれないが，②1つの国に長くいるほど，（その国の）人々がどのように意思疎通を図るかなど，より微妙な違いに多く気づくだろう。

　例えば，イタリアでは電車内で2人が話しているのを見れば，2人が大きな声で話し，身振り手振りが多いので，口論していると思うかもしれない。イタリア語を理解しなければ，2人がただどこで夕食を食べるかを話し合っていることがわからないだろう。別の国では，知らない人の立つ位置があなたから近すぎたり，または遠すぎたりすることを感じるかもしれない。③文化には話している人同士の距離はどれくらいが安心できるかについての不文律がある。

　研究者によると，話している人同士の距離が近い国で知られているアルゼンチンでは，知らない人同士が話す際，互いの平均距離は約0.76メートルである。一方，ルーマニアでは，安心できる距離は1.4メートルまで広がり，アルゼンチンの2倍近くである。コミュニケーションは話す言葉だけでなく，言葉を使わずに行うコミュニケーション，つまり非言語的コミュニケーションでもあることは明らかである。

　アイコンタクトも非言語的コミュニケーションの1つである。北アメリカの大学に留学している日本人学生は，キャ

ンパス内で知らない人が時には何気なくあいさつする時でさえ，目を合わせてくることに驚くことが多い。対照的に，日本の大学に通う北アメリカの学生は，キャンパス内の学生は目を合わせることで人に気づくわけではないように見えるため，愛想がないように思えて驚く。お分かりのように，このような文化の違いに気づかないと，④混乱や誤解につながる可能性がある。

　外国語を話すことはコミュニケーションの一部にすぎない。ある文化での非言語的コミュニケーションのパターンを認識することでずっと効果的に意思疎通を図ることができる。

Lesson 2 (pp.12-19)
Want a Pet? How about a Capybara?

Part 1　基本問題

1(1) used to　(2) awfully

(3) can　(4) can　(5) in the

2(1) for　(2) To start[begin]

(3) of　(4) on

3(1) Drinking milk helps a baby sleep

(2) I picked up an underwater plant

(3) Do you know herbivorous animals only

(4) Where on earth did you go

4(1)(例)You will have an unbelievable experience.

(2)(例)Capybaras can stay underwater for 5 minutes.

(3)(例)When on earth did you come here?

(4)(例)I can't find the key(s). Can you help me look for it[them]?

Part 2　基本問題

1(1) grove　(2) vitamins

(3) stuff　(4) For　(5) or

2(1) choosy　(2) eater

(3) synthesize　(4) diet

3(1) wait for us in a pretty quiet room

(2) suppose they can eat any kind of plant

(3) My son cuddles up with the dogs

(4) People get vitamin C from eating fresh vegetables

4(1)(例)Can we keep[have] capybaras as pets?

(2)(例)They are the same as us humans.

(3)(例)Having a healthy diet every day is not easy.

(例)It is not easy for everyone[people/us] to have a healthy diet every day.

(4)(例)Eat food with vitamin K every day.

Part 3　基本問題

1(1) on　(2) least　(3) predators

(4) come　(5) feel

2(1) knows　(2) depends

(3) put, aside　(4) timid

3(1) I thought jaguars were strong animals

(2) bet her story made him laugh

(3) you know dogs like being petted

(4) say that cats are pretty social animals

4(1)(例)I said "Yes" in a loud voice to get everyone's attention.

(2)(例)More likely, they don't eat other animals.

(3)(例)They may look ridiculous, but they are serious.

(4)(例)Animals in zoos can live twice as long as ones in the wild.

Part 4　基本問題

1(1) in　(2) for

(3) of　(4) to　(5) of

2(1) mammals　(2) pretty much

(3) rodents　(4) for students to

3(1) I don't think my dog bites people

(2) You mean those animals like being together

(3) Wasn't there something about monkeys

(4) kids love to gather around their mothers

4(1)(例)Living in a big[large] family was hard.

(例)It was difficult for me to live in a big [large] family.

(2)(例)You[We] are not allowed to have[keep] a pet in this apartment.

(3)(例)It will be difficult for him to drive to Tokyo.

(4)(例)I saw capybaras swim[swimming] in a hot spring.

Grammar　練習問題

1(1) ③　　(2) ①　　(3) ④　　(4) ③　　(5) ②

2(1) can hear　　　　(2) have, check

(3) It is, to see　　　(4) helped, carry

(5) feel, attracts　　　(6) It isn't, for, to

(7) may start[begin]　　(8) Let, take

(9) made, laugh

3(1) I cannot allow my young son to take such a risk

(2) will make you feel better in a short time

(3) We see a lot of people walk across the busy road

(4) It is natural to want to see the performance

(5) You may put aside this problem

(6) I will let you know the result

(7) I used to hear small children sing and talk

(8) It is impossible for me to read several reports

(9) I like feeling seasons change

(10) Can you have your students come

4(1)(例)You cannot be too careful

(2)(例)Let me think about it

(3)(例)It is fun for me to learn English.

(4)(例)made him quit his job

(5)(例)Have you ever heard a bird sing

(6)(例)help me wash（do）the dishes

(7)(例)My mother made me clean my room.

発展問題

(1) あなたはペット業界の最新の流行の一部は驚くべきものだ[最近の流行には驚くべきものもある]と思うかもしれない。

(2) ② イ　　　③ エ　　　④ ウ

(3) エ　　　(4) 理解力，映像，活動

(5) ア，エ

＜全訳＞

今日，なぜペットはそんなに高価なのか。

ペットを飼うことはいつも今日ほど費用がかかるわけではなかった。以前は，ペットフードを買ったり，グルーミングをしたり，年1回，獣医を受診させたりすることが通常の主な出費であった。最近，ペットの飼い主は最愛のペットにますますお金をかけている。あなたはペット業界の最近の流行には驚くべきものもあると思うかもしれない。それらを見てみることにしよう。

あなたがもし犬を飼うなら，犬はたくさん運動することが必要なので，犬の飼い主の間では散歩がよく行われる。だが，散歩以外のことがしたいなら，実際に飼い犬とヨガをすることができる。これはドーガと呼ばれる。②ドーガを大変気に入っている人たちは，ドーガはペットとのつながりを強くし，飼い犬がリラックスし，健康を維持するのに役立つので，有益であると言う。

⑤今日，餌について，ペットの飼い主には多くの選択肢があり，その多くが非常に高額である。ペットのサイズや好みに特別に合わせた餌を送付する定期サービスを提供する会社もある。ペットが楽しんだり，ごほうびがもらえるようにおやつやおもちゃが入った小包を月1回配送する会社もある。ペットフード市場は間違いなく年々成長している。

ペット用カメラは日中にペットの様子をチェックしたい多くの飼い主にすでに非常に人気がある。だが，飼い主がいない間に犬に何かすることを与えようとする，あるサービスがある。それは⑥DOGTVと呼ばれ，基本的には犬の

理解力に合うように順応させた映像を配信するものである。そのサービスは犬に学ばせることができるプログラミングも備わっているとも主張する。

　今では，飼い主が休暇で出掛ける時，ペットの宿泊施設に払わなければならない金額が高くなった。ペット用ホテルが人が泊まるホテルより費用がかかることもある。ペット用ホテルに泊まっている間，さらにお金を払ってマッサージ，泡風呂，リラックス用の音楽をかけるなどのオプションを選ぶこともできる。

　お分かりのように，今日では簡単にペットに多くのお金をかける。人はペットにお金をかけすぎると思うだろうか。私たちはペットがこれらの特別扱いをどう思っているか決して知ることはないかもしれないが，結局，人は自分のペットにお金をかけるのが好きなようである。

Lesson 3　　　　　　　　　　（pp.20-27）
Grace Darling

Part 1　基本問題

1(1) lighthouse　(2) who
　(3) mostly　　(4) run　　(5) warmth

2(1) deal with　　　　(2) loved
　(3) circular[round]　(4) Victorian

3(1) live in an old house with a wooden staircase
　(2) was one of the first media heroines
　(3) spent most of his life with his parents
　(4) was to warn people away from the fire and smoke

4(1)(例) This room functions as (a) kitchen and (the) living room.
　(2)(例) The road wound up the mountain.
　(3)(例) The light kept burning through the night.
　(4)(例) She was a young brave lady[woman] who lived in Britain.

Part 2　基本問題

1(1) talking　　(2) spray
　(3) nearby　　(4) narrow
　(5) raised

2(1) away from　　(2) balanced
　(3) seek　　　　(4) partly wrecked

3(1) have to bow when our teacher bows to us
　(2) whipped her hair into her eyes
　(3) cut his finger with a jagged rock
　(4) lifted high out of the threshing water

4(1)(例) All the seamen were safe.
　(2)(例) The wind is howling today.
　(3)(例) This ship brings supplies to that island once a week.
　(4)(例) Seagulls are known as violent birds in the United States[America].

Part 3　基本問題

1(1) firmly　　(2) for　　(3) off
　(4) pause　　(5) frightened

2(1) briefly　　(2) in a
　(3) Confirm　　(4) cruel

3(1) as he pulled his clothes over his head
　(2) helped me get my boat into the water against
　(3) I cannot go without him to row the boat
　(4) were almost in hand's reach of the rock

4(1)(例) She turned away from me.
　(2)(例) No one else was speaking[talking] then.
　(3)(例) On a[the] rock alone, he was calling out to me.
　(4)(例) He said, "I must go", but I said, "You must not go."

Part 4　基本問題

1 (1) by　　　(2) princess

(3) nervously　(4) waving

(5) into

2 (1) stumbled　(2) on my own

(3) rather than　(4) fame

3 (1) showed them where they should sit

(2) We consider it important to be kind

(3) closed the door to keep the storm out

(4) dropped the oars in the water when rowing

4 (1)(例)He glanced quietly at me.

(2)(例)I was moved by their skillful performance.

(3)(例)Your duty is to guard[protect] my son.

(4)(例)She sang with tears in her eyes.

Grammar　練習問題

1 (1) ②　(2) ①　(3) ③　(4) ②　(5) ④

2 (1) with his arms folded

(2) find it difficult to work with him

(3) which[that] explains the company well

(4) Did you watch the exciting game?

(5) with his cap in his hand

(6) think it best

(7) whose bag you picked up yesterday

(8) with our mouth full

(9) written in Spanish

3 (1) I consider it important to share the information

(2) The park that is next to ABC Building is called Adela Park / [The park that is called Adela Park is next to ABC Building]

(3) The girl running at the head is my daughter

(4) She was sitting with her coat on in front of

(5) She does not think it so difficult to deal with the issue by herself

(6) This is the point (on) which everyone agrees (on)

(7) We still have some calendars painted

(8) She said goodbye with tears in her eyes

(9) I find it more convenient to go to work by bike

(10) select the person who you think should become a leader

4 (1)(例)I need some boiled eggs

(2)(例)Enter the room with your shoes off.

(3)(例)I think it wonderful to spend all your life

(4)(例)The questions that she asked

(5)(例)We saw him walking across the street.

(6)(例)I'm lonely with you away.

(7)(例)Do you consider it a duty to

発展問題

(1) ウ

(2) 彼女は人形劇の舞台として使うため，自分の家の食卓に穴をあけることさえした。

(3) 当時(Reiniger が初めての映画を発表した頃)のアニメ制作はすべて手作業で行わなければならなかったこと。

(4) 1点目：(アニメーションの父と言われる) Walt Disney の最初の長編アニメ映画よりも彼女の最初の映画の方が先に公開されていたから。

2点目：彼女はアニメーション技術の発展に大きく貢献したから。

(5) イ，エ

＜全訳＞

アニメ制作の母は誰か

2016年6月2日にグーグルのサーチエンジンを調べたならば，短いアニメ映画を見ただろう。映画はロッテ・ライニガーというドイツ人女性についてのもので，彼女が制作した美しいアニメ動画の操り人形の影絵がコンピューターのスクリーン中を踊っているのを見ただろう。ライニガーは1981年に①亡くなったが，この映画は彼女の生誕117周年ということで放映されていた。ロッテ・ライニガーとは誰で，彼女のアニメ制作とのつながりは何だったのか。彼女はあまり知られていないが，彼女のアニメ作品はウォルト・ディズニーの作品より10年早く制作されたため，彼女はアニメ制作の母と考えられるかもしれない。

ライニガーのアニメ制作では彼女が厚くて黒い用紙から切り抜いた操り人形の影絵を用いた。幼い頃から彼女は影絵の切り抜きをつくる技術に②とても興味があった。彼女はよく数時間かけて紙のキャラクターをつくり，それを使って両親に白雪姫などのおとぎ話を形を変えてお話しした。③彼女は人形劇の舞台として使うため，自分の家の食卓に穴をあけることさえした。

多くの人が1936年にウォルト・ディズニーが白雪姫と七人のこびとを公開したため，彼が初めて長編のアニメ映画を製作したと思っている。だが，実はアクメッド王子の冒険というタイトルのライニガーの最初の映画が1926年に公開された。④今日のアニメ映画の製作過程と全く異なり，当時の作品はすべて手作業で行わなければならなかった。彼女は友人の車庫をスタジオとして使って映画の各コマのデザインも，動画制作も，撮影も行った。全工程が終了するまでに5年かかった。

映画製作において，彼女はウォルト・ディズニーを含むその後のアニメーターの創造性を刺激する技術を開発した。彼女は色を使って，映画に陰影をつけて，多彩な背景をつくった。だが，最も重要なこととして，彼女は自分のアニメ動画に深みを与えるカメラを設計した。それまでは，1度に1つの画像しか撮影しなかったため，アニメ動画が平坦であった。新たなカメラでは，彼女はさまざまな水平面に画像を積み重ね，後ろから光をあてながら，上からすべての画像を撮影した。後にウォルト・ディズニーは白雪姫を制作する時にこの技術を使い，カメラはマルチプレーンカメラとして有名になった。

最近，ソーシャルメディアのおかげで，ライニガーの魔法のようなアニメ作品がついに人気になりつつある。新たな世代は多くの人がウォルト・ディズニーがアニメ制作の父であると考えるが，実はアニメ制作技術の発展に大きく貢献したため，ロッテ・ライニガーをアニメ制作の母と見ることができることに納得している。

Lesson 4 (pp.28-35)
Soccer and Foreign Languages

Part 1　基本問題

1 (1) come　　　　　(2) in
　(3) increasingly　(4) popularity
　(5) had

2 (1) Thus　　　　　(2) association
　(3) established　(4) Globalization

3 (1) The car has begun to move slowly
　(2) is studying math hard to prepare for
　(3) MLB stands for Major League Baseball
　(4) a soccer player has been the most desired professional career

4 (1)(例)American society is too competitive.
　(2)(例)That[This] is a significant [important / serious] problem[issue] for us.
　(3)(例)He has become a competent English speaker.
　(4)(例)Small healthy habits make a big difference to[in] your life

Part 2　基本問題

1 (1) studying　　　(2) overseas
　(3) professionally　(4) recall
　(5) Portuguese

2 (1) agent　　(2) a few
　(3) which　(4) long term

3 (1) player has a good command of English
　(2) has played (abroad) in three professional soccer clubs abroad
　(3) which he had filmed in his car
　(4) language is a key to success in foreign

soccer clubs

4(1)(例)There was no need for verbal communication then.

(2)(例)My uncle has been working for a prestigious company for ten years.

(3)(例)My mother, who lives in London, sent me a letter.

(4)(例)The earth, which moves around the sun, is called a planet.

Part 3　基本問題

1(1) charge　(2) of　(3) founded

(4) globally　(5) improve

2(1) concept　(2) metropolitan

(3) selfless　(4) nurture

3(1) have never received any financial aid from

(2) get a lot of information by making use of the Internet

(3) The purpose of my continuing endeavor is to enter a

(4) cultivated his communication skills by meeting many people

4(1)(例)The company provided us with(the) important information.

(2)(例)The number of our branches has increased up to 200.

(3)(例)I had never seen such tall buildings until I moved to Tokyo.

(4)(例)They founded[established] UNICEF, which helps poor children.

Part 4　基本問題

1(1) Moreover　(2) actively

(3) throughout　(4) with

(5) other than

2(1) perfume　(2) linguistic

(3) equipment　(4) Lab

3(1) reputable companies have something in common

(2) not the only athlete who values foreign language skills

(3) anyone other than Kiyoshi see

4(1)(例)Her sister was assigned to the Kobe branch.

(2)(例)He is[has been] regarded as the best soccer player in his class.

(3)(例)I go to a soccer school that[which] nurtures the next generation.

(4)(例)I have been studying hard for six years (in order[so as]) to realize my dream.

(例)I have been studying hard for six years (in order) to make my dream come true.

Grammar　練習問題

1(1) ④　(2) ①　(3) ③　(4) ④　(5) ②

2(1) How long has

(2) have wanted, for

(3) than, had expected

(4) has been, since

(5) which, had bought

(6) have just been

(7) has talked, once

(8) had been, for

(9) have never been

3(1) My daughter has gone abroad to help

(2) told me that Keita had not yet arrived (yet)

(3) How long have they been repairing the copy machine

(4) There have been many problems regarding global warming

(5) The train had already left when we got to the station

(6) because she had been taking me around for hours

(7) Three ways have been considered to solve the issue

(8) How many times have you heard from Karen

(9) whose new book I finished reading

(10) Have you signed up for the English lesson yet

4 (1)(例)which rarely happens

(2)(例)Have you ever taken a subway abroad?

(3)(例)I had never thought about (our) divorce

(4)(例)I had been watching

(5)(例)We have known each other since we were children[since childhood].

(6)(例)she had taken there

(7)(例)which all his friends don't know [none of his friends know(s)]

発展問題

(1) being postponed / participating / bringing / followed

(2) why

(3) 最初の目標：イギリスと同様のスポーツ教育をフランスの学校で生徒にもたらすこと。

その後の夢：近代オリンピックを復活させること。

(4) He was convinced that sports had the power to make world peace

(5) took place　　(6) ア, エ

<全訳>

なぜオリンピックではフランス語が使われているのか

感染症の世界的流行のため，1年間の延期後，2021年夏，東京2020オリンピック・パラリンピック競技会がついに開催された。7月23日，開会式は最大68,000人の観客を収容するために建設された東京の国立競技場で行われた。感染症の世界的流行のため，そこでは小さな群衆が1つできたのみであった。だが，世界中の数百万の人々がテレビで開会式を楽しむことができた。

開会式での伝統の1つは各国のパレードである。各参加国のチームメンバーが自国の国旗を掲げてスタジアムに入場する。東京2020オリンピックでは，205カ国が代表選手を送り，各チームがスタジアムに入場すると，アナウンスが3回行われた。最初にフランス語で，次に英語で，3番目が主催国の言語である日本語で行われた。英語は世界で最も広く話される言語であるが，①なぜフランス語が使われたのだろうと思うかもしれない。その理由は1896年に開催された最初の近代オリンピック競技会までさかのぼることができる。

近代オリンピックの創始者はフランス人男性のバロン・ピエール・ド・クーベルタンであった。彼は常にスポーツ，特にイギリスの教育におけるスポーツ体系に興味を持っていた。元々，彼の目標は同様のスポーツ教育をフランスの学校の子どもたちにもたらすことであったが，結局，彼の展望はそれを超えて，古代オリンピック競技会を復活させるという夢にまで広がった。②彼はスポーツには世界平和を成す力があることを確信していた。

その後，彼は国際オリンピック委員会(IOC)を設立し，1896年，ギリシャで14カ国が集まり，最初の近代オリンピックが開催された。競技会では合計241人のアスリートが43種目で競った。

1898年頃，クーベルタンがオリンピック憲章と呼ばれる公式文書を作成し，その後のオリンピック競技会を開催するルールを明確に記した。憲章23条でいずれのアナウンスも最初にオリンピック競技会の公式言語であるフランス語で行い，次に英語で行うことと記している。その後に主催国の言語が続くことになった。

オリンピック競技会に関連する伝統は多く，フランス語の使用はそのほんの1つである。次にアナウンスを聞く時，オリンピックを近代に持ち込むという考えを持っていたピエール・ド・クーベルタンという男性のことを思い起こしてみよう。

Lesson 5 (pp.36-43)
Raising Awareness of Disadvantaged People

Part 1 基本問題

1 (1) untrained　　(2) challenged

　(3) mentally　　(4) outsider

2 (1) A large number of　(2) lover

　(3) be expected　　(4) painting

3 (1) You can put on some music if

　(2) lies in its simple but powerful

　　expressions

　(3) which exhibits beautiful glass works

　　inside

　(4) They will display foreign cars for sale

4 (1)(例) I have seen a member of the Royal

　　Family of Japan.

　(2)(例) Her pencil drawings are popular

　　among foreigners.

　(3)(例) An art museum is a place where you

　　can see art exhibitions.

　(4)(例) That bread may be made by people

　　with special needs.

Part 2 基本問題

1 (1) disabilities　(2) formal

　(3) surprise　　(4) where

2 (1) outstanding　(2) as well

　(3) decades　　(4) how

3 (1) none of them could receive proper

　　education

　(2) the institution where children with

　　special needs

　(3) Thursday is the day when I take a piano

　(4) everyone should have a right to

　　education

4 (1)(例) The singer received [won / got] two

awards last year.

　(2)(例) Her debut as an actress was in 1992.

　(3)(例) I work for a higher education institution.

　(4)(例) With or without disabilities, we all

　　have human rights.

Part 3 基本問題

1 (1) in　　(2) variety

　(3) supporter　　(4) documentary

　(5) In

2 (1) participate　(2) annually

　(3) accommodate　(4) distinct

3 (1) I felt tired when I was working on

　(2) earnestly thought we would be invited

　　to

　(3) had an argument about a monetary

　　problem

　(4) Aki did not attempt to go outside

4 (1)(例) Let's think about social welfare.

　(2)(例) This company makes a variety of

　　[various] products.

　(3)(例) Check the picture[photo] attached

　　to the email.

　(4)(例) What are the requirements to enter

　　the institution?

Part 4 基本問題

1 (1) secondary　(2) facilities

　(3) childcare　　(4) disabled

　(5) anniversary

2 (1) foundation　　(2) independence

　(3) commitment　　(4) integrated

3 (1) taught us the importance of self-reliance

　(2) raise money to support welfare for weak

　　people

　(3) She is still active in caring for those people

(4) started as a small private care home

4 (1) (例) The founder of the building is my grandfather.

(2) (例) This work should be done [completed / finished] by tomorrow.

(3) (例) There are many [a lot of] magazines which [that] look back on the 20th [twentieth] century.

(4) (例) Due to (some) monetary trouble(s), it became difficult to run the school.

(例) It became difficult to run the school due to (some) monetary trouble(s).

Grammar　練習問題

1 (1) ③　　(2) ②　　(3) ④　　(4) ②　　(5) ①

2 (1) should be finished

(2) point where

(3) standing looking

(4) That is how

(5) must be loved [liked]

(6) year when

(7) will be completed

(8) How

(9) looked surprised

3 (1) can see the whole stage from where you are sitting

(2) don't remember how I came home from far away

(3) Your mobile phone must not be used during the lecture

(4) why so many people try to hurt others with SNS

(5) This summer heat makes us feel exhausted

(6) Are there any places where we can park our cars

(7) Can many stars be seen here

(8) The night is when most of us go to bed

(9) have become worried that he has got lost

(10) since he sat crying alone

4 (1) (例) where I can use my experience

(2) (例) (The reason) Why I'm calling

(3) (例) The magazine should be found

(4) (例) got injured [wounded] in the accident

(5) (例) The time will come when

(6) (例) The event may be canceled

(7) (例) show you how the machine works

発展問題

(1) ア

(2) 学校のホームグラウンドでフットボールの試合が行われる，テーマ

(3) A オ　B イ

(4) ウ

(5) gave me a chance to appreciate the experiences I had there

(6) ウ

＜全訳＞

アメリカでの高校時代の思い出

　私は前にアメリカを訪れた時，かつて通った高校に立ち寄った。かなり長い年月を経て再び学校の入り口に入るのは変な感覚であった。歩き回ると，思い出があふれ，「高校は楽しかったかい」と自問自答した。その答えは一心に考えなければならなかったが，結局，私は①大変な時があったが，素晴らしい思い出もたくさんあることに気づいた。

　学校での最も楽しかった週の1つは②ホームカミングウィークであった。そう呼ばれるのは，その週の終わりに学校のホームグラウンドでフットボールの試合が予定されたからであった。それに向けて生徒を活気づけるため，試合前の1週間は「スピリットウィーク」と決められ，1日ごとに違うテーマが設けられた。例えば，ある日は「おかしな帽子をかぶる日」で，別の日は「カウボーイのような格好をする日」であった。試合日にチアリーダーによる演技があるため，生徒全員が体育館に集まった。翌日はそこ

で音楽をかけるために DJ が雇われたり，または地元のバンドが生演奏したりする気軽なダンスパーティーが開かれた。

その1年での別の大きなイベントとして，毎年春にプロムと呼ばれる正装したダンスパーティーがあった。それはとても大きなもてなしで，皆，誰をデートに誘うかをよく考えた。初めて正装するのはとても楽しかった。男子は高級なタキシードを借り，女子は色鮮やかな正装用ドレスを買って着るのであった。生徒の多くがその夜のためにリムジンを借り，その後自宅でパーティーを開いた。

もちろん，③アメリカの高校はすべて楽しかったわけではなかった。特に良い成績を維持することが重要であった最後の2年間は大きなプレッシャーとなった。学校生活とアルバイトとを両立させることは大変であった。さらに，大学への出願は私的な経験や将来への大望について長いレポートを書くのに大変な労力を要したため，大変ストレスを感じた。

私は久しぶりにゆっくり時間を取って自分の高校を訪れてうれしかった。④高校を訪れ，私がそこで得た経験をありがたく思い，私がそれからどれほど変わったかを実感する機会を得た。私は数年後，必ずまた戻ってこようと思う。

Lesson 6 (pp.44-51)
Problems Behind Self-Driving Cars

Part 1　基本問題

1 (1) in　(2) ourselves

(3) in　(4) lanes

2 (1) jam　(2) vehicle

(3) shortage　(4) What's more

3 (1) video chat function can be useful

(2) Will our mother allow us to eat

(3) are those who can speak three languages

(4) the auto button on the coffee maker

4 (1)(例)Do you know anyone who has a self-driving car?

(2)(例)I want you to deal with that customer.

(3)(例)I will be busy preparing for dinner this evening.

(4)(例)It is said[They say] that the new technology will reduce car[traffic] accidents.

Part 2　基本問題

1 (1) imagine　(2) oncoming

(3) crash　(4) if

2 (1) highway　(2) edge

(3) programmer　(4) cliff

3 (1) the ocean on the left side

(2) If you go into the opposite lane

(3) We were traveling down the street

(4) You need to make a quick decision

4 (1)(例)Go straight and (then) turn right.

(2)(例)If I were rich, I could live in Los Angeles.

(3)(例)A car accident happened, and I got thrown onto the road.

(4)(例)Turning left here means that you'll kill many people.

Part 3　基本問題

1 (1) automatically　(2) possibility

(3) may　(4) criminal

2 (1) involved　(2) emergency

(3) justified　(4) fatal

3 (1) a truck ran over a kangaroo on the road

(2) not harm the environment under any circumstances

(3) a chance of getting hit by a car

(4) are programmed to avoid those who are walking

4 (1)(例)His story cannot be true.

(2)(例)Taka got[was] involved in a car [traffic] accident.

(3)(例)They are considered[regarded] as

criminals.

(4)(例)If you had a million yen, what would you buy?

補充問題

1 (1) practicing　(2) were

(3) cannot　(4) wish

2 (1) made, decision　(2) People

(3) ran over　(4) allowed, to

(5) What's more

3 (1)(例)先生は私たちに教科書を見ないように忠告しました。

(2)(例)あなたは高速道路を運転するのを難しいと思うかもしれません。

(3)(例)母は8時前に家を出たので，今頃はもう仕事場についているはずです。

(4)(例)もし曲がり角を逃して崖から落ちたらどうしますか？

(5)(例)あなたがもし彼ならどうやってその意見を正当化しますか？

Grammar　練習問題

1 (1) ④　(2) ②　(3) ①

2 (1) cannot be　(2) advised, not to

(3) caused, to be

(4) were, would

(5) be forced to

(6) reminds, to check

(7) were not raining, should[would]

(8) can make　(9) not allowed to

(10) wish I could　(11) warns, not to

3 (1) The participants are required to fill out the application form

(2) would appreciate it if you could give me some information

(3) who allows her staff members to decide

things by themselves

(4) might feel better if you could sleep well

(5) shouldn't be difficult to imagine our life without mobile phones

(6) Shall we persuade her to be a member of our development team

(7) would happen to us if we didn't take the offer

(8) afraid that I may catch a cold

(9) important to encourage children to have a lot of experiences

(10) would you spend your days if you had enough time and money

(11) urged our company to reconsider the plan

4 (1)(例)me to turn on the heater

(2)(例)tell the resident not to

(3)(例)would you buy if you were me

(4)(例)I wish I didn't have to go to work today.

(5)(例)She should get to the office in an hour.

(6)(例)Jane must know where she is.

発展問題

(1) 給料，労働時間

(2) ウ

(3) 従業員がより満足すれば，従業員の生産性が上がり，従業員はその会社により長くとどまること。

(4) 勤務時間，会社の建物から出る

(5) エ，カ

＜全訳＞

　素晴らしい職場をつくるのは何か

　大人になったら何になりたいですか。あなたは小学生の時，この質問にどう答えましたか。プロのアスリートになるか，花屋やパン屋で働きたかったですか。①高校や大学

14

を卒業するまでには，あなたの仕事への願望はかなり変わるかもしれない。職を選ぶには給料や労働時間などの多くのことを考える必要があるが，最近の就職希望者は職を決める際に職場環境も考慮する。

この点で，テクノロジー企業は②職場環境を社員にとって魅力的なものにすることに重点的に取り組んできた。テクノロジー企業は楽しくて，心地よく仕事ができる職場をつくろうとする。

例えば，巨大テクノロジー企業であるグーグルはその職場文化で知られている。その理念は社員がより満足すれば，社員の生産性が上がり，社員はその会社により長くとどまるというものである。それは③お互いにとってプラスになる状況である。そういう理由で，グーグルのオフィス環境は社員の満足度を念頭に置いてつくられるのである。

よくグーグラーと呼ばれるアメリカのグーグル本社に勤務する社員は，多くのサービスが無料で提供されるため，通常，勤務時間に社外に出る必要はない。社員は社屋内にいくつかある喫茶店やレストランはどこでも楽しむことができる。④これにより時間を節約するだけでなく，社員は日中にお互い交流しやすくなる。

グーグラーが歯のクリーニングのため，歯医者に行く時間がなかったら，社屋内に歯科クリニックがあり，社員は予約できる。社員が週末にどうしても髪を切りに行けなくとも，グーグル本社にはフルサービスの美容室があるので，問題ではない。社員が長時間のコンピューターでの作業により肩が凝れば，マッサージのサービスが利用できる。

このようなサービスに加え，社員の息抜きも優先される。休憩が必要な社員は特別に設計されたスリープポッドで仮眠を取ったり，卓球をしたり，最新のテレビゲームを試すことができる。フィットネスセンターや水泳プールもあり，社員はそこで運動できる。

このような職場をつくっているのはグーグルだけではない。フェイスブック，ネットフリックス，アマゾンなどの他のテクノロジー企業も職場環境改善に投資してきた。企業は競って最も優秀な社員を獲得するため，就職希望者にとって職場環境は重要な検討事項になりつつある。

Lesson 7 (pp.52-59)
An Inspiring Figure in Modern Japan

Part 1 基本問題
1 (1) preparatory　(2) naturalist

(3) scholar　　　(4) classics

(5) historical

2 (1) reference　(2) wildlife

(3) specimens　(4) On the table

3 (1) America is made up of fifty

(2) you should add milk bit by bit

(3) Among her classmates were Joe

(4) is the country where I was born

4 (1)(例) I don't like coffee either.

(2)(例) When I was a student, I was not good at memorizing.

(3)(例) I read a book written in the Edo period.

(例) I read a book which was written in the Edo period.

(4)(例) She will[is going to] graduate from an agriculture college this year.

Part 2 基本問題
1 (1) scholarship　(2) religious

(3) journals　(4) faith

(5) biology

2 (1) behavior　(2) intelligence

(3) contributed　(4) revolutionists

3 (1) is a very quiet boy by nature

(2) His enthusiasm for baseball has changed

(3) foreign languages, including Greek and Latin[Latin and Greek]

(4) she may lose her temper over this

4 (1)(例) I have found a temporary job.

(2)(例) His curiosity (has) brought him to this school.

(3)(例) My achievement at the company got a lot of attention.

(4)(例) The museum exhibits more than one million handicrafts.

Part 3　基本問題

1(1) fungus　　(2) object to

　　(3) writings　　(4) poorly

　　(5) formally

2(1) author　　(2) weaken

　　(3) insist　　　(4) proper

3(1) contributed the result of her research to

　　(2) That thing over there seems to be

　　(3) Single-celled creatures have the nature of

　　(4) concern was to make a decision

4(1)(例)Ken was named after his grandfather.

　　(2)(例)I don't want you to get[be] arrested
　　　　　by the police.

　　(3)(例)I want to become[be] a person who
　　　　　can contribute to society.

　　(4)(例)We aim to combine two different
　　　　　religions.

Part 4　基本問題

1(1) inspiring　　(2) Despite

　　(3) surprisingly　(4) Ecology

2(1) Ministry　　(2) Emperor[emperor]

　　(3) conservation　(4) glory

3(1) offers free lectures on plants

　　(2) a specimen of slime mold

　　(3) put them in old candy boxes

　　(4) at the wildlife reserve on the island

4(1)(例)I couldn't recognize my old friend(s).

　　(2)(例)This rock is a National Treasure of
　　　　　the prefecture.

　　(3)(例)In addition to his fame, he gained
　　　　　honor.

　　(4)(例)The good news made us happy.

Grammar　練習問題

1(1) Into the pool jumped the swimmer.

　　(2) Here comes Kenta

　　(3) It seems that Kate has a good time
　　　　dancing.

　　(4) The book doesn't seem to be written in
　　　　English.

　　(5) It seems that she has forgotten[forgot]
　　　　my name.

2(1) enabled, to　　(2) made

　　(3) At, center, is

　　(4) It seemed, were

　　(5) delighted　　(6) didn't surprise

　　(7) Under, runs

　　(8) doesn't seem to

　　(9) led to　　　(10) gave

3(1) What prevented them from starting
　　　　their business

　　(2) It didn't seem that the two researchers
　　　　had the same opinions

　　(3) A few minutes' walk from here will bring
　　　　you to the city hall

　　(4) around the corner is the library

　　(5) That picture reminds me of the day

　　(6) This handout made it easy for the
　　　　students to understand the class

　　(7) We seem to have no choice but to rely
　　　　on him

　　(8) his left stood his mother with flowers

　　(9) The news didn't show us whether

　　(10) We don't seem to be able to keep up
　　　　with the pace

4(1)(例)The storm caused a delay

　　(2)(例)seem to have lost your textbook

　　(3)(例)the room rushed out a boy

　　(4)(例)doesn't allow him to tell a lie

　　(5)(例)It seems that he is in a hurry to
　　　　　catch a train.

(6)（例）What made him quit his job suddenly?

(7)（例）seems to have been false

発展問題

(1) ボラカイ島への観光客の数が（大幅に）増えたため，島の美しさがほぼ完全に破壊されたこと。

(2) The lack of sewage and waste treatment facilities

(3) 1日に島に入ることを許可される観光客の数を（6,405人に）限定したこと。

(4) 島に到着した人は登録されたホテルに泊まることを証明するために，ホテルの予約[ホテルを予約していること]を示すことも義務付けられた。

(5) ウ，エ

＜全訳＞

ボラカイ島とオーバーツーリズム

　ボラカイ島はフィリピンの小さな島で，総陸地面積は10.32km平方キロメートルである。島の長さは7kmしかなく，最も幅が狭い地点は1kmに満たない。1970年代始め，観光客が島の静かな青緑色の海や白い砂浜に惹かれ，ボラカイ島は徐々に人気の目的地となった。残念ながら，かつては「地上の楽園」と呼ばれた島は数十年に及ぶ環境被害に耐えた後，2018年に観光客に対して閉鎖された。

　1980年代を通じて，ボラカイ島に旅行する観光客の数は着実に増えた。その後，高級ホテルがオープンし始め，観光客の数は2000年の26万人から2009年には65万人に急増した。2012年，島は有名な旅行雑誌によって「最高の島」を授与され，観光客が増加し，同年は120万人を受け入れた。2017年までに200万人以上の観光客があり，多すぎる観光客が原因で島の美しさはほぼ完全に破壊された。これが①観光公害と呼ばれる。

　多すぎる観光客，②不十分な社会基盤，政府による法律施行の失敗でボラカイ島は環境災害地域となった。下水や廃棄物の処理施設がないことで，重大な健康問題が引き起こされた。例えば，ボラカイ島の最も人気のある砂浜は水質汚染がひどく，皮膚感染や胃の不調を引き起こした。さらに，監視のないシュノーケリングや違法な魚釣りにより，

島のサンゴ礁の約70%が破壊された。

　2018年，フィリピン大統領のロドリゴ・ドゥテルテは島の環境の緊急事態を宣言し，その後6カ月間，島を閉鎖した。その間，島を再建する活動が完了した。効率的な新たな下水処理システムが建設され，将来に向けての持続可能な観光事業を確実にする計画がたてられた。

　島が開放されると，③いくつかの新しい方針が導入された。最も重要なこととして，1日に島に入ることが許可される観光客の数が6,405人に制限された。④島に到着した人は登録されたホテルに泊まることを証明するために，ホテルの予約（ホテルを予約していること）を示すことも義務付けられた。使い捨てのプラスチックの使用は完全に禁止された。

　観光公害は世界中の多くの観光目的地にとって重大な問題である。希望として，政府は「観光事業が栄えるほどよい」という観光事業モデルを再考し，私たちが自然の美しさを守りながら観光スポットを楽しみ続けることができるように，持続可能な将来を確実なものとする政策を打ち出すだろう。

Lesson 8 （pp.60-67）
A New Symbol of Singapore

Part 1　基本問題

1(1) futuristic　　(2) specialist

　(3) Antarctica　　(4) grows

2(1) the tropics　　(2) Mediterranean

　(3) conservatory　　(4) olives

3(1) to everyone except for me

　(2) changed their house into a restaurant

　(3) measure up to 50 meters tall

　(4) requires cold temperatures to bear fruit

4(1)（例）Then[At that time], his shirt was soggy.

　(2)（例）The college[university] was built on reclaimed land.

　(3)（例）The structure of that building saves water and energy.

　(4)（例）How much will it cost to landscape this site?

Part 2 基本問題

1 (1) magical   (2) instantly

   (3) synchronize   (4) architecture

2 (1) trunk   (2) concrete

   (3) Living   (4) using

3 (1) plays an important role in our body

     function

   (2) took cues from some novels from

   (3) The giant Karri trees in Australia are

   (4) are recognizable as symbols of Singapore

4 (1)(例)For collecting[To collect] the sun's

     [solar] energy, it has many branches.

   (2)(例)I had a sense of wonder from(by)

     watching the movie.

   (3)(例)That equipment acts as an air exhaust.

   (4)(例)My mother cooks, listening to music. /

     [Listening to music, my mother cooks.]

Part 3 基本問題

1 (1) glass   (2) steel

   (3) arch   (4) on

2 (1) Roman   (2) Made

   (3) ideal   (4) column

3 (1) has been used for electronic products

   (2) who made the world's first greenhouse

   (3) our lunch time in this way

   (4) let the ball through his legs

4 (1)(例)The view from the top of this tower

     is amazing[great / wonderful].

   (2)(例)I hid in the shadow of a tree because

     it was too hot.

   (3)(例)Built two years ago, the house looks

     new.

   (4)(例)Written in Chinese, the book was

     hard to understand (for me).

Part 4 基本問題

1 (1) subtropical   (2) Typically

   (3) savings   (4) in

2 (1) Organic   (2) misty

   (3) On   (4) humidity

3 (1) Having lived in Australia for two years

   (2) can result in a weight gain

   (3) an amazing collection of plant life

   (4) They gathered those from all over

4 (1)(例)I[We] could see wild animals up close.

   (2)(例)I want to[would like to] learn[know]

     more about energy saving technology.

   (3)(例)His job[duty] is to fix[repair] broken

     water pipes.

   (4)(例)All things considered, I[we] cannot

     say she is wrong.

Grammar 練習問題

1 (1) Knowing well how to deal with

    emergencies,

   (2) If[When] it is seen from the roof of the

    hotel,

   (3) She introduced herself briefly, beginning

    a speech.

   (4) Not studying so hard,

   (5) If we climb to the top of the mountain,

   (6) Having already finished my homework,

   (7)(例)Don't use your mobile phone when

    [if] you drive your car.

    (例)Don't use your mobile phone when

    [while] you are driving your car.

   (8) Not having had breakfast,

   (9) opened the bottle and poured the orange

    juice into my glass.

   (10) Surrounded by flowers,

   (11) Since[After] he had failed several times,

2 (1) calling my name

(2) Having

(3) Not being busy

(4) Strictly speaking

(5) All things considered

3 (1) Talking with my friend on the phone, I noticed

(2) Poor in his childhood, he was tough and bright

(3) I bowed to him, thanking him for his help

(4) Asked to attend the meeting for him, can you

(5) Admitting your proposal, we cannot cooperate

(6) Never having been to France, she is proficient in French

4 (1) (例) always keeping his promise

(2) (例) Not feeling well,

(3) (例) Having seen her many times,

(4) (例) Judging from my experience,

(5) (例) Weather permitting,

発展問題

(1) ① エ　　④ イ

(2) シンガポールに行くことになって初めて

(3) 新たな科学技術[テクノロジー]，軽量の素材

(4) ア　　(5) ウ

＜全訳＞

世界最長の直航便での飛行！

数年前，私は大学時代からの友人からメールをもらった。彼女は卒業後に仕事のため，シンガポールに移ったが，私たちはまだ①連絡を取り合っていた。メールは彼女の結婚式への招待状であった。彼女はシンガポールで出会いがあり，２人はその年末にシンガポールの高級ホテルの１つでの結婚式を計画していた。なんて心躍らせる知らせなのだろう。私はすぐにメールで彼女の記念すべき日のためにシンガポールに行くと返事した。

②シンガポールに行くことになって初めて，私は「どうやってシンガポールに行くのだろう」と考えた。当時，私はニューヨーク市に住んでいたため，インターネットを検索して入手可能なチケットについて知った。驚いたことに，③飛行時間はとても長く，19時間であった！私はニューヨーク市に近いニュージャージー州のニューアーク・リバティー国際空港からのシンガポール航空の便を予約した。その後，私は当時，その便は世界最長の直航便で，約10,000マイルに及ぶことを知った。

幸運にも，チケットをビジネスクラスに上げるためにマイレージサービスを使うことができた。エコノミークラスで19時間過ごすのはまったく④魅力的に思えなかった。私は機内でそんなに長時間過ごすことにワクワクもすれば，不安にもなった。2013年に初めてそのルートの飛行が行われたが，燃料費が高いため数年後に廃止になったことを私は知った。私がそのルートを利用するまでには，燃料費は下がり，航空機を製造するのに新たな技術と軽量の素材が使われたことにより航空機が再びそのルートを飛行することが可能になった。

ついに出発日となり，私は搭乗手続きのため空港に向かった。機内では提供される食べ物の種類の多さに驚いた。私が客室乗務員の１人に話しかけると，彼女は私に機内にシェフがおり，飛行中，合計480のメニューの組み合わせが可能であると教えてくれた。

ビジネスクラスの座席は快適で，1200時間分の内容の最新のエンターテイメントシステムが備わっていた。ノートパソコンに適した，引き出して使うデスクがついており，広い座席は平坦なベッドに変えることができた。実際に私は少し眠ることができ，19時間後にシンガポール・チャンギ国際空港に到着した時，すがすがしい気分であった。

友人の結婚式では楽しい時間を過ごしたが，⑤世界最長の航空便での経験も忘れられないものであった。シンガポールは訪れるには興味深い都市で，またいつか来てみたいと思う。

Lesson 9　　　　　　(pp.68-75)
Reaching for New Rocks

Part 1　基本問題

1 (1) Dr.　　　(2) production

(3) imagery　(4) spacecraft

2 (1) astrophysics　(2) exists

　　(3) composer　(4) Imperial

3 (1) taller than any other building

　　(2) an astrophysicist who has joined NASA

　　(3) no longer considered as a planet

　　(4) more distant from here than any other

4 (1)(例)You can see the horizon from there.

　　(2)(例)They revealed the truth to everyone except him.

　　(3)(例)It was hard (for me) to write this thesis.

　　(4)(例)In this way,[This is how(the way)] she became a doctoral student.

Part 2　基本問題

1 (1) attractions　(2) thrill

　　(3) of　(4) portrait

2 (1) exploration　(2) flyby

　　(3) mid-August　(4) rhyme

3 (1) you to put together the two images [put the two images together]

　　(2) released a song to celebrate their friends'

　　(3) was invited to be present on

　　(4) how inspiring the whole project was

4 (1)(例)I was wondering if I can rely on him.

　　(2)(例)On any occasion, she works hard.

　　(3)(例)You can take stereo pictures with a smartphone.

　　(4)(例)This movie seems[looks] less interesting than the one (that) we saw[watched] yesterday.

Part 3　基本問題

1 (1) down　(2) take

　　(3) on　(4) As

2 (1) submit　(2) admitted

　　(3) physics　(4) literally

3 (1) up your room in the first place

　　(2) often wonder what makes us unique

　　(3) song brought her back to TV

　　(4) has clearly shown that he is

4 (1)(例)I want to finish writing my doctoral thesis by tomorrow.

　　(2)(例)We should work on the[our] homework right now.

　　(3)(例)Please tell me[us] about the solar system.

　　(4)(例)Do you know if[whether] we have a test tomorrow?

Part 4　基本問題

1 (1) interact　(2) recordings

　　(3) were　(4) had known

2 (1) legacy　(2) tombstones

　　(3) come across

　　(4) could have avoided

3 (1) was married to a Japanese woman

　　(2) the very top of their game

　　(3) Watching the flyby of the spacecraft

　　(4) celebrations were beamed out to the world

4 (1)(例)We (will) go to our grandparents' house on New Year's Day.

　　(2)(例)It was traveling four billion miles (away) from Earth.

　　(3)(例)If I had been free last night, I would have gone out with you.

　　(4)(例)Public attention was on Voyager 2, which had come back to Earth.

Grammar　練習問題

1 (1) No (other) city in Japan is more crowded than Tokyo.

(2) Nobody (else)〔No one (else)〕plays a more important role than Mr. Nakamura in saving lives.

(3) If the weather had been good, the event would have been successful.

(4) If you had not been with me, I couldn't have put up with the anxiety.

(5) If she had been angry, I would have gone to see her in person.

2 (1) Nothing, more

(2) care if〔whether〕

(3) had not sent, couldn't have arrived

(4) should have told

(5) No other, more

(6) wondering whether〔if〕

(7) would have happened, had not found

(8) better than any other test

3 (1) had explained the rule, we might have taken less time

(2) Nothing is more effective than gargling

(3) Time will tell whether you are right or wrong

(4) there had not been his fine play, our team would have lost the game

(5) I'm not sure if he said such a thing

(6) has performed longer than any other member

(7) could have met the client for her if she had asked me

(8) No other company is more famous than

(9) Would you judge whether the person is appropriate

4 (1)（例）If you had known my phone number, could you have called me earlier?

(2)（例）I want to ask the expert whether the experiment was successful (or not).

(3)（例）We should not have turned left at the corner.

(4)（例）me know if you are interested in joining 〔entering〕 our company

(5)（例）If he had followed his teacher's advice, he could have passed the exam.

(6)（例）has more functions than any other cellphone

(7)（例）I doubt if〔whether〕 something so strange〔such a strange thing〕 can really happen.

発展問題

(1) those

(2) （アラン・フリードという）ラジオのディスクジョッキーが（1950年代に）初めてクリーブランドで「ロックンロール」という（用）語を使ったから。

(3) ウ　　(4) イ　　(5) ア　　(6) イ

＜全訳＞

ロックンロール音楽に捧げられた博物館

　オハイオ州クリーブランドのロックの殿堂博物館はロック音楽の歴史を賛美し，長年，そのジャンルの発展に重要な役割を果たした人々の貢献を讃えている。博物館の場所として検討された都市はいくつかあったが，②最終的に選ばれたのはクリーブランドであった。多くの人がその理由はアラン・フリードというラジオのディスクジョッキーが1950年代に初めてクリーブランドで「ロックンロール」という用語を使ったからだと考えている。

　博物館を訪れると，他の博物館と同様，有名なミュージシャンが使った楽器，ステージ衣装，歌詞が書かれたページ，オリジナルのアルバム作品，ポスター，写真などの③ゆかりの物がずらりと展示されている。博物館には広範囲に及ぶ研究図書館もある。

　ロックの殿堂に選出されるには，アーティストの最初のレコーディングから25年が過ぎている必要がある。毎年，ロックの歴史家による委員会により候補者が選ばれる。その後，約500人のロックの専門家による国際的な団体が投

票して，最高投票数を得た人が殿堂入りする。毎年，5〜7名のミュージシャンがその栄誉を得る。毎年，ニューヨーク市で公式のセレモニーとコンサートが開催され，多くの殿堂入りメンバー自身の生演奏により新たなメンバーを讃える。

2021年現在，338名のアーティストが殿堂入りした。1986年の最初の殿堂入りグループの中にはエルヴィス・プレスリーやレイ・チャールズなどのスーパースターが含まれた。最初の女性アーティストの殿堂入りは1年後のアレサ・フランクリンの選出であった。他の有名な殿堂入りメンバーには2001年のマイケル・ジャクソンや2020年のホイットニー・ヒューストンがいた。

ロック音楽の歴史は短いが，ロックの殿堂博物館は皆がこれまでの音楽業界にとってとても重要なミュージシャンを記憶する場所としての役割を果たす。今あなたが好きなミュージシャンの中で誰が殿堂入りすると思いますか。⑤それは誰にもまったくわからない。

Lesson 10 (pp.76-83)
The Power of a Woman's Will to Make Changes

Part 1 　基本問題

1(1) unfairly　　(2) A

　(3) unknown　　(4) equality

2(1) much, than　　(2) Gender

　(3) unsung　　　　(4) achieved

3(1) only need to look closely enough

　(2) and poor people is becoming wider

　(3) has long been promoted as a

　(4) shows that Japan came in 40th in

4(1)(例)It is going to rain nationwide tomorrow.

　(2)(例)Nowadays[Today], more and more foreigners are visiting Japan.

　(3)(例)What the teacher said yesterday was very impressive.

　(4)(例)She is a 44-year-old elementary school teacher.

　　(例)She is an elementary school teacher who is 44 years old.

Part 2 　基本問題

1(1) fair　　　　　(2) sponsorship

　(3) Philippines　(4) distinguished

2(1) orphanage　　(2) financial

　(3) Cambodia　　(4) accessory

3(1) Some craft fairs will be held

　(2) her key chain in her neighborhood

　(3) sponsor for my visa to stay in Germany

　(4) looking for a donor for their baby

4(1)(例)Locally grown vegetables are cheap.

　(2)(例)We take care of the baby[babies] in turn.

　(3)(例)I cannot speak English, much less French.

　(4)(例)This website was specially designed for foreigners.

Part 3 　基本問題

1(1) Furthermore　　(2) welcomed

　(3) intangible　　　(4) in

2(1) Poverty　　(2) educate

　(3) cooperate with

　(4) non-profit

3(1) conduct research on mental health

　(2) must support less privileged people

　(3) By joining these expensive tours

　(4) to raise awareness of gender equality

4(1)(例)My mother never drives.

　(2)(例)His cousin is getting taller and taller.

　(3)(例)The injured man could hardly [scarcely] walk.

　(4)(例)That company develops teaching materials for teachers in Japan.

Part 4 　基本問題

1(1) happiness　　(2) freshman

(3) overcome　　(4) underprivileged

2(1) divorced　　(2) fortunate

(3) Psychological　　(4) identified

3(1) attempt failed in the end

(2) Now that the storm is gone

(3) seen each other for a while

(4) effort turned out to be a great

4(1)(例)I could hardly hear your voice.

(2)(例)(Please) prove who is right.

(3)(例)I asked my father if[whether]

marriage is a good thing.

(4)(例)Tom rarely[seldom] drinks (sake).

Grammar　練習問題

1(1) more, more

(2) can hardly[scarcely]

(3) rarely[seldom] changes

(4) has never been

(5) less and less

(6) is seldom[rarely] used

(7) further and further

(8) never to

(9) worse and worse

2(1) makes it easier and easier to get

information

(2) There are scarcely companies without PCs

(3) Never betray others unless you want to

lose trust

(4) grow angrier and angrier each time we

remember the fact

(5) is so bright that she hardly makes the

same mistake

(6) The sky turned darker and darker

because of the storm

(7) the area was scarcely affected by the

heavy rain

(8) Is the need for bilingual people becoming

greater and greater

(9) Important matters are rarely determined

by one member

(10) never dreamed that I would be promoted to

(11) customers complain about are seldom

improved

(12) is quiet and scarcely speaks to anyone

(13) Is it true that Westerners seldom take a

bath

3(1)(例)become more and more eager to

increase her vocabulary

(2)(例)I'll never forget the message

(3)(例)they will get better and better at it

(4)(例)She practiced harder and harder

(5)(例)She never fails to exceed our

expectation(s).

(6)(例)My father is hardly[scarcely] at home

on weekends.

(7)(例)I rarely[seldom] see a dentist

(8)(例)We never get tired of listening to great

music.

(9)(例)I can hardly wait for the concert to

start.

(10)(例)Never be afraid of trying something

new.

発展問題

(1) 男女平等を達成し，すべての女性と少女に

権利を与える

(2) 大臣職の50%以上を女性が務めていること。

(3) エ

(4) 1つ目：インドの地方議会で，議会が女性

主導である地域の飲用水プロジェ

クトの数が，議会が男性主導の地

域より 62% 高い。

2つ目：ノルウェーでは，市議会に女性がいることが児童保護の利用率が上がることと直接関連がある。

(5) ア

＜全訳＞

政治における女性の役割

2015年，193カ国が2030年までに達成することを誓う17の持続可能な開発目標(SDGs)を採択した。5番目のSDGは「男女平等を達成し，すべての女性と少女に権利を与える」ことである。①この目標に向かってまい進するために，政治における女性の役割を増やすことが不可欠である。世界中での女性の政治参加に関する現況を見てみよう。

2021年現在，世界で女性が国家元首である国は22カ国しかなく，日本を含む119カ国で女性に国のリーダーを任せたことがなかった。今日，ニュージーランドのジャシンダ・アーダーンのような女性リーダーが増えることが若い女性にとって重要な模範となる。

政府の大臣については，女性は世界全体のわずか21%にすぎない。②男女均等を達成している，つまり大臣職の50%以上を女性が務めている国は14カ国しかない。日本では，菅首相のもと，閣僚に選ばれた女性は2名しかおらず，これより前の安倍政権の3名から減少した。

国会では女性の割合は25%しかなく，50%を達成しているのは4カ国しかない。アフリカの国であるルワンダが61%と世界一で，キューバとボリビアがいずれも53%である。40%以上を達成している国は合計19カ国で，そのうち9カ国がヨーロッパ，5カ国がラテンアメリカとカリブ海，4カ国がアフリカ，1カ国が太平洋にある。

女性の政治参加が盛んな多くの国が施行してきた政策の1つは③性別による定数である。その政策により，選挙に立候補するのに必要な女性候補者数を定めるか，または政治団体での女性のための議席を一定数確保する法律がつくられる。

④より多くの女性が政治に参加することは政策の観点から有益であることが証明されている。例えば，インドの地方議会に関する調査で議会が女性主導である地域の飲用水プロジェクトの数が議会が男性主導の地域より62%高いことが判明した。ノルウェーでは研究者により市議会に女性がいることが児童保護の利用率が上がることと直接関係があることが判明した。

5番目のSDGに述べられる目標を達成するにはまだ大きく進歩しなければならないことは明らかである。だが，いくつかの国が女性の政治参加に成功したことで，より多くの国が目標に向かってより速く進むことが期待される。これは確実に女性のみでなく，社会全体に利益をもたらすだろう。

NOTE

NOTE

NOTE

Ambition English Communication I
Workbook
解答・解説

BD

開隆堂出版株式会社
東京都文京区向丘1-13-1

Ambition

English Communication I

Workbook

開隆堂

このワークブックは,「Ambition English Communication Ⅰ」の内容に沿って作られています。教科書で扱われた Lesson 1 から 10 の Grammar を中心に対応しており,構文の理解をねらいとしてさまざまな形式の問題で構成してあります。各 Lesson は,構文の理解を目標とした基本問題,知識の定着に役立つ練習問題,大学受験への橋渡しとなる発展問題から構成されています。また,巻末には教科書に掲載された単語や熟語の一覧なども掲載していますので,毎日の授業の予習だけでなく,復習や定期テスト前の整理にも役立ちます。各ページの内容と使い方は次のとおりです。

●基本問題

教科書各 Lesson のパートごとに問題を掲載しています。試験でよく問われる最頻出問題を厳選して紹介していますので予習に適しています。さまざまな出題形式から構文を練習できるよう工夫しておりますので,定期テスト対策としても役立ちます。一度解いた問題も何回も音読すると定着も早く進みます。

●練習問題

教科書の Grammar のページに対応しています。教科書の Grammar の学習を補強できるよう,また実際の試験問題の形式に慣れるよう,本冊を繰り返し解いて知識を定着させましょう。

●発展問題

大学受験への準備となるよう本課で扱った題材を別な視点から扱った長文問題を掲載しています。長文は本書用に書き下ろしたオリジナルなので,時間を計るなど試験のつもりで解くとよいでしょう。

目次

1　Choose the correct answer.

(1)　Our rent increased by three times (in / at) the beginning of April.

(2)　I heard the news shortly after (returning / returned) home.

(3)　The doctor said that you (will / would) get better soon.

(4)　I was very (shocking / shocked) when my grandmother died.

(5)　Our duty is (for / to) make the maximum profit.

2　Fill in the blanks to complete the sentences.

(1)　そのテストに申し込むには一連の手続きが必要です。

You need (　　　　) (　　　　) (　　　　　　) procedures to apply for the test.

(2)　アシスタントとしてこれ以上私の講義に遅刻をするとクビになりますよ。

If you are late for my (　　　　　　) again as an assistant, you will be fired.

(3)　管理者の視点から，問題をみてみましょう。

Let's look at the problem from the manager's (　　　　　　).

(4)　毛布と食料が避難した人々に配られました。

Blankets and food have been (　　　　　　) to people who evacuated.

3　Reorder the words in brackets so that they can make sense.

(1)　He is (a / conservative / degree / to / certain).

_____

(2)　What is (of / talking to / him / the / use)?

_____

(3)　(as / the principal / his duty / of the school) is to make his students happy.

_____

(4)　If you don't work hard, (ought / scold / you / to / your boss).

_____

4　Translate the Japanese into English.

(1)　その映画はとてもつまらなかったです。

_____

(2)　彼は放課後，家で勉強します。

_____

(3)　私は友達と話すためにカフェに行きました。

_____

(4)　私の母は手紙を書くことが好きです。

_____

1 Choose the correct answer.

(1) Please write (up / down) your answer on the answer sheet.

(2) My mother left me a piece of (papers / paper).

(3) I cannot accept this increase (in / on) rent.

(4) He went up the stage and then proceeded to (give / giving) a speech.

(5) The baseball game made us (exciting / excited).

2 Fill in the blanks to complete the sentences.

(1) 新しい車が欲しいですが，買う余裕はありません。

I want to get a new car, but I can't (　　　　　) it.

(2) 日本の平均年収は約 400 万円です。

The average annual (　　　　　) in Japan is about 4 million yen.

(3) 太陽光発電の欠点は，日照量に影響されるということです。

A (　　　　　) of solar power is that it is affected by the amount of sunlight.

(4) 見出しの下の 1 文目は非常に大事です。

The first sentence under the (　　　　　) is extremely important.

3 Reorder the words in brackets so that they can make sense.

(1) (English / Ms. Tanaka / us / taught) last year.

_____

(2) You will have the big hall (for / to / free / rent / the musical).

_____

(3) What did you (of / yesterday / to / do / instead / going / school)?

_____

(4) On the other hand, you (may / good chance / money / to / some / make / a / lose).

_____

4 Translate the Japanese into English.

(1) 実際，ミキと私はその時間に家にいました。

_____

(2) このプロジェクトには多くの利点があります。

_____

(3) 彼は明日そこには行かないだろうと言いました。

_____

(4) 収入を増やすことはそれほど簡単なことではありません。

_____

5

1   Choose the correct answer.

(1) My friend is working for an (advertised / advertising) company.

(2) The painting (is worth / worths) a lot of money.

(3) It has two advantages. One is profitability and (another / the other) is accessibility.

(4) Please read the documents (carefully / careful).

(5) They achieved their goals without (to make / making) a lot of effort.

2   Fill in the blanks to complete the sentences.

(1) 念の為に言っておくけど，これは会社の重要な情報です。

(   ) you, this is important information of the company.

(2) 全ての質問に答え終わったら，必ず見直しをしてください。

When you finish answering all the questions, please make sure to (   ).

(3) 政府は貧しい人々の為に家賃の引き上げの減額を計画しています。

The government is planning a (   ) of the rent increase for poor people.

(4) その手紙は家賃が3倍に上がることを示していました。

The letter indicated that the rent (   ) be increased 300 percent.

3   Reorder the words in brackets so that they can make sense.

(1) (final / gave / me / he / decision / his) by the deadline.

_____

(2) The teacher (of / the sheet / the student / paper / handed / to).

_____

(3) The writer (as / the show / is / as / its / of / actors / well-known).

_____

(4) (attract / to / people / crowds / those lectures / of / intelligent) the hotel.

_____

4   Translate the Japanese into English.

(1) 私はそれを受け取り，次の日彼に返事をしました。

_____

(2) インターネットには多くの利点と欠点とがあります。

_____

(3) 私たちは駅への行き方を話しました。

_____

(4) その会社は新聞広告を出し始めました。

_____

1 Choose the correct answer.

(1) What do you mean by (to raise / raising) our rent 200 percent?

(2) The girl cried for the toy until her parents finally gave (in / up).

(3) (At / In) a glance, I found that he was not older than me.

(4) He plays tennis as (well / good) as soccer.

(5) I realized that I was wrong, but I didn't back (up / down).

2 Fill in the blanks to complete the sentences.

(1) 私の昇給はわずか時給 10 セントでした。ばかげてないですか？

My pay raise was only 10 cents per hour. Isn't it (　　　　　)?

(2) その答えはとても単純で明快です。

The answer is so simple and (　　　　　).

(3) たとえ雨が降っても私たちは公園へ行きます。

We will go to the park even (　　　　　) it rains.

(4) 私は留学することについて母と議論しました。

I had an (　　　　　) with my mother about studying abroad.

3 Reorder the words in brackets so that they can make sense.

(1) You (about / to / talk / your / ought / it / with / parents).

_____

(2) (have / an / we all / ability / with / to / connect) others.

_____

(3) What is (on / education / of / your / view / online / point)?

_____

(4) It is often (see / to / the other / important / person's / angle / from / things).

_____

4 Translate the Japanese into English.

(1) このコーヒーは熱すぎて飲めません。

_____

(2) 彼女は私にいくつかのいいアドバイスをくれました。

_____

(3) 彼らは試験に合格するためにとても一生懸命勉強しました。

_____

(4) 地球上の 9 割の人間はそれを無視するだろうと彼は思いました。

_____

1 Choose the correct word from ① to ④ to fill in the blank.

(1) Umbrellas (　　　) well on a rainy day.

　① buy　　　　② sell　　　　③ lose　　　　④ purchase

(2) Let's (　　　) the issue at the meeting.

　① discuss on　② discuss to　③ discuss about　④ discuss

(3) He changes his job frequently (　　　) new experiences.

　① having　　② to have　　③ have　　　④ has

(4) I often (　　　) our city library.

　① visit　　　② visit to　　③ go　　　　④ come

(5) I look forward to (　　　) part in the annual picnic.

　① be taking　② take　　　③ taking　　④ have taken

2 Fill in the blanks to complete the sentences.

(1) 私は寒気がするので，風邪をひいているに違いありません。

　I must have a cold because I (　　　　　) (　　　　　).

(2) 彼はささいなことでよく怒ります。

　He often (　　　　　) (　　　　　) at something trivial.

(3) 適度な運動で私たちは健康を保つことができます。

　A proper amount of exercise can (　　　　　) (　　　　　) healthy.

(4) 彼らは会議の準備で忙しかったです。

　They were (　　　　　) (　　　　　) for the conference.

(5) 何か食べる物を持ち寄りましょう。

　Let's bring something (　　　　　) (　　　　　).

(6) 私はその時はその問題を簡単に解決できると思いました。

　I thought that I (　　　　　) solve the problem at that time.

(7) 1時間前に雨がやみました。

　It (　　　　　) (　　　　　) an hour ago.

(8) 私は駅へ急ぎましたが，結局，電車に間に合いませんでした。

　I rushed to the station, (　　　　　) (　　　　　) miss the train.

(9) 私は普段，朝食をとる前にシャワーをあびます。

　I usually take a shower (　　　　　) (　　　　　) breakfast.

3 Reorder the words in brackets so that they can make sense.

(1) (of / safe / that / us / all members / happy / were / the news / made / the group).

_____

(2) Our first goal (many / to / unknown cultures / introduce / is) around the world.

_____

(3) First, (taught / to / us / our English teacher / use a dictionary / how).

_____

(4) (you / will / the ticket / I / get) if you have no time to go to the ticket office.

_____

(5) I (could / relieved / my son / to / arrive there / hear / was) in time.

_____

(6) (at / are / expressing / not / Japanese people / their opinions / good).

_____

(7) (my pet cat's / it's / to / fun / reaction / me / see / for) to the toy.

_____

4 Translate the Japanese into English.

(1) 彼女は欲しいものをうまく手に入れました。(succeed を使って)

_____ what she wanted.

(2) 彼女はその本をとても退屈だと思いました。(found を使い，5 文型の形で)

_____

(3) 私の弟は何度も試験を受けて，弁護士になりました。

_____ after taking exams many times.

(4) 食べ過ぎて私は眠くなりました。(動名詞を使い，文型の形で。眠い = sleepy)

_____

(5) 彼女はそのことを決して人には言わないと言いました。

_____ tell it to others.

(6) 私は後悔しないために最善を尽くしたいです。(最善を尽くす = do one's best)

_____ not to regret.

(7) 私はしなければならない宿題がまだたくさんあります。

I still _____ .

(8) 交通渋滞のため，バスは3時まで来ません。

_____ until 3 o'clock due to the traffic jam.

(9) あなたの隣に座ってもいいですか。(mind を使って)

_____ next to you?

(10) 私の夢は退職後に故郷に戻ることです。(動名詞を使って)

_____ my hometown after retirement.

9

Deeper Understanding of Communication

Visiting foreign countries allows you to ①experience their cultures firsthand. Though you can study cultures by reading books or watching videos on the Internet, setting foot in a country and noticing the cultural differences yourself is much more interesting. Of course, the most obvious differences might be things like the language, food, and the

5　way people dress, but ②the longer you spend in a country, the more you'll notice more subtle differences such as how people communicate.

In Italy, for example, when you see two people talking on a train, you might think they are arguing because they are speaking in loud voices and gesturing a lot. Without understanding Italian, you wouldn't know that they were simply discussing where to

10　have dinner. In other countries, you might feel that strangers stand either too close or too far from you. ③Cultures have unwritten rules about what distance is comfortable between speakers.

In Argentina, known to be a country of close-talkers, the average distance between strangers speaking is about 0.76 meters according to researchers. In Romania, on the

15　other hand, the comfortable distance expands to 1.4 meters, nearly double that of Argentina! Communication is clearly not only about the words you use, but also the communication that takes place without words, or nonverbal communication.

Eye contact is another part of nonverbal communication. Japanese students studying abroad at universities in North America are often shocked when strangers make eye

20　contact with them on campus, even sometimes greeting them casually. In contrast, students from North America attending Japanese universities are surprised that people seem unfriendly because students on campus don't seem to acknowledge others by making eye contact. As you can see, being unaware of such cultural differences can lead to ④confusion and misunderstandings.

25　Speaking another language is only a part of communication. Becoming aware of the nonverbal communication patterns in cultures can make you an even more effective communicator.

(316 words)

10

(1) 下線部①は具体的にどうすることか，文脈に応じて日本語で答えなさい。

_____

(2) 下線部②を日本語にしなさい。

_____

_____

(3) 下線部③を言い換えた次の英文の空所に，文脈に応じて適切な語句を補い，文を完成させなさい。

Whether someone talks (　　　　　) to or (　　　　　) from you depends on her or his (　　　　　).

(4) 下線部④を説明する英文として正しいものを1つ選び，記号で答えなさい。

ア　Japanese students studying at universities in North America are trying hard to greet strangers casually.

イ　Japanese students studying abroad in North America are not used to how people communicate there.

ウ　Students from North America in Japan become unfriendly because their eye contact is rejected there.

エ　Students from North America in Japan can adjust to the Japanese way of communication soon.

(　　　)

(5) 本文の内容と一致するものを1つ選び，記号で答えなさい。

ア　It is better to learn with books and the Internet before going abroad to feel cultural differences directly.

イ　Italians tend to argue about trivial matters such as where they eat.

ウ　Communication consists of not only verbal communication but also the ways without words.

エ　We should start with learning another language to be effective communicators.

(　　　)

1　Choose the correct answer.

(1)　I (am used to / used to) have a guinea pig at home.

(2)　We need an (awful / awfully) big cage for them.

(3)　You (will / can) hold a frog in your hand, but snakes are too big for that.

(4)　Mike (will / can) use chopsticks well because he lived in Japan for one year.

(5)　Capybaras live (in the / in a) wild.

2　Fill in the blanks to complete the sentences.

(1)　どうして牛は4つの胃袋を持っているのですか。

What do cows have four stomachs (　　　　　　)?

(2)　先ず，お越しいただきましてどうもありがとうございます。

(　　　　　　) (　　　　　　　　) with, thank you so much for coming.

(3)　今日はたくさんの人に会ったので疲れました。

I got tired because I saw plenty (　　　　　　) people today.

(4)　パンダは笹を食べて生きています。

Giant pandas live (　　　　　　　) bamboo leaves.

3　Reorder the words in brackets so that they can make sense.

(1)　(helps / sleep / drinking / milk / a baby) well.

_____

(2)　(an / up / picked / underwater / I / plant) for my research.

_____

(3)　(you / animals / do / only / herbivorous / know) eat plants?

_____

(4)　(go / on / did / where / earth / you)? We were looking for you.

_____

4　Translate the Japanese into English.

(1)　あなたは信じられないような経験をするでしょう。

_____

(2)　カピバラは水中に5分間いることができます。

_____

(3)　一体全体いつここに来たのですか。

_____

(4)　鍵が見つかりません。探すの手伝ってくれませんか。

_____

1 Choose the correct answer.

(1) We walked through a (glove / grove) of trees to come here.

(2) This fruit has a lot of (fat / vitamins).

(3) You have a lot of (stuff / staff) to do today.

(4) That's crazy. (To / For) one thing, you never told me that it's my duty.

(5) You should eat more vegetables or fruit, (or / and) you'll get sick.

2 Fill in the blanks to complete the sentences.

(1) 僕の妹は食べ物の選り好みをします。

My sister is (　　　　　　) about food.

(2) 彼は少食でしたが，今はよく食べます。

He used to be a small (　　　　　　), but now he eats a lot.

(3) 人間の体はアミノ酸を合成することはできません。

The human body cannot (　　　　　　) amino acids.

(4) バランスの取れた食事をとることはとても大切です。

Having a balanced (　　　　　　) is very important.

3 Reorder the words in brackets so that they can make sense.

(1) You can (a / wait / room / us / in / pretty / for / quiet).

_____

(2) I (kind / they / suppose / any / eat / of / can / plant).

_____

(3) (up / the dogs / with / my / cuddles / son) every night.

_____

(4) (from / get / fresh / vitamin C / vegetables / eating / people) and fruit.

_____

4 Translate the Japanese into English.

(1) カピバラをペットとして飼うことはできますか。

_____

(2) 彼らは私たち人間と同じです。

_____

(3) 健康な食事を毎日とることは容易ではありません。

_____

(4) ビタミンKを含む食べ物を毎日食べなさい。

_____

1 Choose the correct answer.

(1) Japanese women live for eighty years (in / on) average.

(2) You should study at (less / least) two hours after school.

(3) Jaguars are (predators / supporters) for most animals.

(4) How (come / go) you said such a thing?

(5) Drinking hot tea makes me (to feel / feel) better.

2 Fill in the blanks to complete the sentences.

(1) さあ，どうでしょう。もしかすると，あとでこれが必要になるかもしれません。

　　Who (　　　　　　)? Perhaps you may need this later.

(2) それは場合によると思います。

　　I suppose it (　　　　　　).

(3) 毎月老後のためにいくらかお金をとっておきましょう。

　　Let's (　　　　　) some money (　　　　　) for our retirement every month.

(4) 臆病な動物を捕まえることはライオンにとって容易でしょう。

　　Catching (　　　　　) animals must be easy for lions.

3 Reorder the words in brackets so that they can make sense.

(1) (strong / I / animals / jaguars / thought / were), but I was wrong.

_____

(2) I (story / him / made / her / bet / laugh).

_____

(3) Do (petted/ know / like / you / being / dogs)?

_____

(4) We can (are / that / animals / cats / social / say / pretty).

_____

4 Translate the Japanese into English.

(1) 全員の注意を引くために大声で「はい」と言いました。

_____

(2) それどころか，それらは他の動物を食べないのです。（相手の意見への応答として）

_____

(3) ばかげてみえるかもしれませんが，彼らは真剣です。

_____

(4) 動物園にいる動物は野生の動物よりも二倍長く生きられます。

_____

1   Choose the correct answer.

(1)   The patients were divided (in / on) age groups.

(2)   Some people have hamsters (by / for) pets.

(3)   Come to think (of / at) it, I have met him before.

(4)   The mother gave a toy (for / to) her child.

(5)   It is kind (for / of) you to invite us to the party.

2   Fill in the blanks to complete the sentences.

(1)   クジラは哺乳類とは知りませんでした。

I didn't know whales are (   ).

(2)   私は彼女におおかた賛成です。

I (   ) (   ) agree with her.

(3)   ところで，ネズミはげっ歯類であっていますよね？

By the way, mice are (   ), right?

(4)   学生が勉強を楽しむことはとても重要です。

It is very important (   ) (   ) (   ) enjoy their studies.

3   Reorder the words in brackets so that they can make sense.

(1)   (think / dog / I / bites / my / people / don't) much.

_____

(2)   (being / you / those / mean / together / like / animals) all the time?

_____

(3)   (about / there / something / wasn't / monkeys) in Japan?

_____

(4)   Of course, (love / around / gather / kids / to / their mothers).

_____

4   Translate the Japanese into English.

(1)   大家族の中で生活するのは大変でした。

_____

(2)   このアパートでペットを飼うことは許されていません。

_____

(3)   彼が東京まで運転するのは難しいでしょう。

_____

(4)   私は温泉でカピバラが泳ぐのを見ました。

_____

1 Choose the correct word from ① to ④ to fill in the blank.

(1) I think you can (　　　) a restroom on the second floor.

　　① finding　　② to find　　③ find　　④ found

(2) Our English teacher often makes us (　　　) a short essay in English.

　　① write　　② writing　　③ to write　　④ written

(3) I see Kate (　　　) the front door every day.

　　① to clean　　② cleans　　③ cleaned　　④ clean

(4) You may (　　　) whether you will take a break before or after me.

　　① choose　　② chooses　　③ decide　　④ decides

(5) (　　　) me take some more pictures.

　　① Give　　② Let　　③ Allow　　④ Get

2 Fill in the blanks to complete the sentences.

(1) 時々，ここから教会の鐘が鳴るのを聞くことができます。

　　We sometimes (　　　　　) (　　　　　) the church bell ring from here.

(2) 私は修理業者に自分のパソコンを見てもらいたいです。

　　I want to (　　　　　) a repair shop (　　　　　) my computer.

(3) 違う視点から物事を見ることは大事です。

　　(　　　　) (　　　　　) important (　　　　) (　　　　　) things from a different viewpoint.

(4) 健太は私が椅子を運び出すのを手伝ってくれました。

　　Kenta (　　　　　) me (　　　　　) the chairs out.

(5) 私たちは日本の良さが外国の方を引き付けるのを感じます。

　　We (　　　　　) the goodness of Japan (　　　　　) people in other countries.

(6) 彼が個人的な質問に答える必要はありません。

　　(　　　　) (　　　　　) necessary (　　　　) him (　　　　) answer personal questions.

(7) 生徒は問題集の分かるところから始めてよいです。

　　Students (　　　　　) (　　　　　) with the part they know well.

(8) 息子が興味があるなら，そのセミナーに参加させましょう。

　　(　　　　) my son (　　　　　) part in the workshop if he is interested in it.

(9) 彼のジョークで私たちは皆笑いました。

　　His jokes (　　　　　) all of us (　　　　　).

3 Reorder the words in brackets so that they can make sense.

(1) (to / cannot / my young son / I / a risk / allow / take / such).

_____

(2) The pill (feel / make / in a short time / better / will / you).

_____

(3) (a lot of / see / the busy road / we / walk across / people).

_____

(4) (the performance / natural / to / is / want to / see / it) of Mr. Ohtani every day.

_____

(5) (put / you / aside / this problem / may) if you have something else to do.

_____

(6) (will / know / I / let / the result / you) as soon as I find it out.

_____

(7) (sing and talk / used to / I / small children / hear) from the house next door.

_____

(8) (to read / me / impossible / for / reports / it is / several) at a time.

_____

(9) (change / like / I / seasons / feeling) and enjoy nature.

_____

(10) (have / come / can / your students / you) early tomorrow morning?

_____

4 Translate the Japanese into English.

(1) 知らない場所を運転する時は，注意してもし過ぎることはありません。

_____ when you drive a car in a strange place.

(2) それについて少し考えさせてください。（Let を使って）

_____ for a moment.

(3) 私にとって英語を学ぶことは楽しいです。（It is を使って。楽しい＝ fun）

_____

(4) 彼はどうしてその仕事を辞めたのですか。（What で始めて。辞める＝ quit）

What _____ ?

(5) あなたは静かな森の中で鳥が鳴くのを聞いたことがありますか。（鳴く＝ sing）

_____ in a silent forest?

(6) お皿を洗うのを手伝ってくれませんか。

Would you _____ ?

(7) 母は私に部屋を掃除させました。

_____

Why Are Pets So Expensive These Days?

Having a pet was not always as expensive as it is today. In the past, buying pet food, getting your pet groomed and a once-a-year visit to the vet were usually the main expenses. Nowadays, pet owners are spending more and more money on their beloved pets. ①You might find some of the latest trends in the pet industry surprising. Let's have a look.

If you have a dog, you know that they require a lot of exercise, so walking is a common practice among dog owners. But if you want to do something other than walking, you can actually do yoga with your dog. It's called doga. Those who ②are into it say it is ③beneficial because it helps ④solidify the bond with their pets and helps dogs relax and stay in shape.

⑤There are a lot of choices for pet owners regarding food these days, many with pretty high prices. Some companies offer subscription services that send food to your pet that has been customized specifically for your pet's size and preferences. There are other companies that send monthly packages with treats and toys to keep your pet entertained and rewarded. The pet food market is definitely growing year by year.

Pet cameras are already quite popular with many pet owners who want to check up on their pets during the day. But one service is trying to give dogs something to do while their owners are away. It's called ⑥DOGTV and it essentially delivers images that are adapted to suit dogs' understanding. The service even claims that some of its programming can teach your dog.

When pet owners go on vacation, they now have to pay higher prices for accommodation for their pets. Sometimes pet hotels can even cost more than those for people. While staying at pet hotels, you can also pay more for options like massage, bubble baths or playing relaxing music.

As you can see, it's easy to spend a lot of money on your pets these days. Do you think people spend too much on their pets? We may never know how pets feel about these extras, but in the end, people seem to love spending money on their pets.

(367 words)

(1) 下線部①を日本語になおしなさい。

_____

_____

(2) 下線部②，③，④の意味に最も近いものを1つ選び、記号で答えなさい。

② ア are worried about it イ like it very much
　 ウ hesitate about it エ understand it well

③ ア abundant イ trivial
　 ウ lucky エ helpful

④ ア ruin イ remove
　 ウ strengthen エ seek for

②(　　　) ③(　　　) ④(　　　)

(3) 下線部⑤の例を示す英文として正しいものを1つ選び，記号で答えなさい。

ア The food that pet owners can purchase at a low expense.
イ The food that is packed with care goods.
ウ The food that is healthy for dogs.
エ The food that fits the features of each dog.

(　　　)

(4) 下線部⑥の特徴を記した次の文の空欄に適切な語句を補いなさい。

DOGTV はペット犬の(　　　　　　　　　　)に応じた(　　　　　　　　　　)を提供すること
で，ペット犬は(　　　　　　　　　)することができる。

(5) 本文の内容と一致するものを2つ選び，記号で答えなさい。

ア There are more choices to do for pets than before.
イ Walking a pet is still the best to keep it healthy.
ウ Pet cameras are popular because pet owners can keep great memories with their pets.
エ Pet hotels gives some services in addition to accommodations.
オ Many items for pets are so expensive that many pet owners give up purchasing them.

(　　　　　　)

1 Choose the correct answer.

(1) We saw a (light house / lighthouse) near the beach.

(2) The man (who / which) was called Mr. Strange was my father.

(3) I lived (most / mostly) in Kanto region before college.

(4) He got a job at the company (running / run) by his father.

(5) They started a fire with wooden materials for cooking and (warmth / warm).

2 Fill in the blanks to complete the sentences.

(1) 私にとってあの車を扱うのは難しかったです。

It was hard for me to (   ) (   ) that car.

(2) これは多くの人に愛されている本です。

This is a book (   ) by plenty of people.

(3) 彼はこのマンションの円い部屋が気に入っています。

He likes the (   ) room in this apartment.

(4) 私はヴィクトリア朝時代の歴史に興味があります。

I am interested in the history of the (   ) era.

3 Reorder the words in brackets so that they can make sense.

(1) I used to (a / old house / in / wooden staircase / live / an / with).

_____

(2) Grace Darling (of / heroines / was / the / media / first / one).

_____

(3) He has (his parents / spent / most / his life / with / of).

_____

(4) The alarm (people / the fire and smoke / was / away / warn / to / from).

_____

4 Translate the Japanese into English.

(1) この部屋はキッチンやリビングとして機能します。

_____

(2) その道は山の上へ曲がって進んでいました。

_____

(3) その明かりは夜通し燃え続けていました。

_____

(4) 彼女はイギリスに住む勇敢な若い女性でした。

_____

1   Choose the correct answer.

(1) Do you know the girl (talked / talking) to the teacher?

(2) Can you pass me the (spray / splay)?

(3) The restaurant is (nearly / nearby) the bank that my brother went to yesterday.

(4) I couldn't move ahead from that point because the road was too (narrow / wide).

(5) We could see their hands (raised / raising) to look for help.

2   Fill in the blanks to complete the sentences.

(1) あなたの犬を私に近づけないで下さい。

Please keep your dog (   ) (   ) me.

(2) バランスの取れた食事とは様々な種類の食べ物を含む食事のことです。

A (   ) diet is a diet that includes different kinds of foods.

(3) 我々は皆幸せを探し求めますが，手にする人は僅かです。

We all (   ) happiness, but very few get it.

(4) この家は地震で一部損壊しました。

This house was (   ) (   ) by an earthquake.

3   Reorder the words in brackets so that they can make sense.

(1) Do we (us / bow / when / to / our teacher / to / have / bows)?

_____

(2) The wind (eyes / hair / into / her / whipped / her).

_____

(3) He (jagged / his finger / a / with / rock / cut).

_____

(4) The ship was (water / of / the / high / lifted / out / threshing).

_____

4   Translate the Japanese into English.

(1) 船乗りは全員無事でした。

_____

(2) 今日は風がヒューヒューと吹いています。

_____

(3) この船は日常必需品をあの島に週一回持っていきます。

_____

(4) カモメはアメリカでは狂暴な鳥として知られています。

_____

1 Choose the correct answer.

(1) The new mayor spoke (firm / firmly) in the public.

(2) I can't believe that they care (of / for) four children.

(3) He was standing (on / off) their cats.

(4) There is a long (pose / pause) in the middle of the song.

(5) I was (frightened / frightening) when I found it.

2 Fill in the blanks to complete the sentences.

(1) 手短に説明して頂けますか？

Could you explain it (　　　　　)?

(2) もうすぐそちらへ行きます。

I'll get there (　　　　) (　　　　　) moment.

(3) あなたが入力したパスワードは正しくありません。パスワードを確認してください。

The password that you entered is incorrect. (　　　　　) your password.

(4) 動物に対して残酷な人は信用できません。

I can't trust people who are (　　　　　) to animals.

3 Reorder the words in brackets so that they can make sense.

(1) He was running down the stairs (his clothes / over / pulled / as / his head / he).

_____

(2) My father (get / against / into / helped / my boat / me / the water) the waves.

_____

(3) (row / I / without / to / him / the boat / cannot go) while I do the rescue.

_____

(4) We (of / reach / were / hand's / in / the rock / almost).

_____

4 Translate the Japanese into English.

(1) 彼女は私から顔を背けました。

_____

(2) その時，他の誰も話していませんでした。

_____

(3) 岩の上で一人，彼は私を大声で呼んでいました。

_____

(4) 彼は「行かなければならない」と言いましたが，私は「行ってはならない」と言いました。

_____

1 Choose the correct answer.

(1) I picked up the coins one (on / by) one.

(2) She was a media (prince / princess) in the 1980s.

(3) He (nervously / nervous) brought the papers to us.

(4) She ran towards me with her hair (waved / waving).

(5) Hollywood turned him (away / into) a movie star.

2 Fill in the blanks to complete the sentences.

(1) 船に乗り込んだとき，つまづきかけました。

I almost (　　　　　　) when I went onto the ship.

(2) もし自分の庭があったなら，たくさんのヒマワリを植えたいです。

If I have a garden (　　　　) (　　　　) (　　　　), I want to plant a lot of sunflowers.

(3) お米よりもむしろ麺が食べたいです。

I would like to eat noodles (　　　　) (　　　　) rice.

(4) 多くの人は成功とは富と名声を手に入れることだと思っています。

Many people think that success is about achieving (　　　　　) and wealth.

3 Reorder the words in brackets so that they can make sense.

(1) My brother (sit / they / them / where / showed / should).

_____

(2) (it / kind / to / consider / important / we / be) to others.

_____

(3) She (out / the door / keep / to / closed / the storm).

_____

(4) They (when / the oars / in / dropped / rowing / the water) a boat.

_____

4 Translate the Japanese into English.

(1) 彼は静かに私を一瞥しました。

_____

(2) 私は彼らの巧みな演技に感動しました。

_____

(3) あなたの仕事は私の息子を守ることです。

_____

(4) 目に涙をためながら彼女は歌いました。

_____

1 Choose the correct word from ① to ④ to fill in the blank.

(1) Do you know the girl (　　　) essay received the first prize of the contest?

　① that　　　② whose　　　③ which　　　④ who

(2) The student (　　　) a flute is my sister.

　① playing　　② plays　　　③ to play　　　④ played

(3) Takao saw the movie with his eyes (　　　).

　① being shining　② shone　　③ shining　　④ shines

(4) I can't find the book (　　　) I have been looking for since yesterday.

　① who　　　② which　　　③ whose　　　④ whom

(5) Who will clear the (　　　) windowpane.

　① breaking　　② broke　　　③ break　　　④ broken

2 Follow the instructions and rewrite the following sentences.

(1) The man was thinking. His arms were folded（with を使って）

　The man was thinking _____.

(2) You will find it is difficult to work with him.（下線部を find O C の形に）

　You will _____.

(3) This is a pamphlet. It explains the company well.（関係代名詞を使って）

　This is a pamphlet _____.

(4) Did you watch the game? It was exciting.（関係代名詞を使わずに 1 つの文に）

　_____

(5) He is running. He is holding his cap in his hand.（with を使って）

　He is running _____.

(6) We think it is best to be silent.（下線部を think O C の形に）

　We _____ to be silent.

(7) Do you remember the boy? You picked up his bag yesterday.（関係代名詞を使って）

　Do you remember the boy _____?

(8) We cannot speak well when our mouth is full.（with を使って）

　We cannot speak _____.

(9) I read a letter. It was written in Spanish.（関係代名詞を使わずに 1 つの文に）

　I read a letter _____.

3 Reorder the words in brackets so that they can make sense.

(1) (to / it / I / important / the information / consider / share).

_____

(2) (next to / is / Adela Park / ABC Building / is / that / called / the park).

_____

(3) (is / at the head / the girl / my daughter / running).

_____

(4) (her coat / she / in front of / was / on / with / sitting) the heater.

_____

(5) (to / think / does not / the issue / it / deal with / she / by herself / so difficult) .

_____

(6) (on / this is / agrees / everyone / the point / which).

_____

(7) (some calendars / have / painted / still / we) in color.

_____

(8) (with / said / in / she / her eyes / goodbye / tears).

_____

(9) (find / go to work / I / to / by bike / more convenient / it) than by car.

_____

(10) Will you (you think / become / select / who / the person / a leader / should)?

_____

4 Translate the Japanese into English.

(1) 私は料理にゆで卵がいくつか必要です。(〜をゆでる = boil)

_____ for cooking.

(2) 靴を脱いで部屋に入ってください。(with を使って)

_____

(3) 人のために一生を費やすことは素晴らしいと思います。(think O C の形で)

_____ helping others.

(4) 彼女が尋ねた質問は的を射ていました。(that を使って)

_____ were to the point.

(5) 私たちは彼が通りを横切っているのが見えました。(現在分詞を使って)

_____

(6) あなたがいなくて寂しいです。(with を使って, いない = away)

_____

(7) あなたは間違ったルールでも従うことは義務だと考えますか。(consider O C の形で)

_____ follow even the wrong rules?

25

Who is the Mother of Animation?

If you had checked Google's search engine on June 2, 2016, you would have seen an animated short film there. The film was about a German woman named Lotte Reiniger and you would have seen her beautifully animated puppet silhouettes dancing across your computer screen. Though Reiniger ①passed away in 1981, this film was being shown
5　because it would have been her 117th birthday. Who was Lotte Reiniger and what was her connection to animation? Though she is not well known, she might be considered the mother of animation since her animated works pre-dated Walt Disney's by 10 years.

Reinger's animation used puppet silhouettes that she cut out from thick black paper. From an early age, she had been ②fascinated with the craft of making silhouette cutouts.
10　She would often spend hours making her paper characters and then use them to retell fairy tales such as Snow White for her parents. ③She even cut a hole in a dining room table at her home so that she could use it as a stage for her puppet shows.

Many people assume that Walt Disney was the first to produce a full-length animated film when he released Snow White and the Seven Dwarfs in 1936. However, Reiniger's first
15　film titled The Adventures of Prince Achmed, in fact, was released in 1926. ④Far different from today's animated film making process, the work in those days had to be done entirely by hand. She both designed, animated, and photographed each frame of the film using a friend's garage as a studio. The whole process took 5 years to complete.

In making the film, she developed technics that would later give inspiration to future
20　animators, including Walt Disney. She used color to tint the film to make multi-colored backgrounds. But most significantly, she designed a camera that gave her animation depth. Up until then, animation was flat because only one image at a time was photographed. For the new camera, she stacked images on different horizontal planes and then photographed them all from above lighting them from behind. Walt Disney would later use this technic
25　when he made *Snow White* and the camera became known as the multiplane camera.

Recently, thanks to social media, Reiniger's magical animated works are finally becoming popular. A new generation is understanding that while many consider Walt Disney to be the father of animation, in fact, Lotte Reiniger could be seen as the mother of animation due to her immense contribution to the development of animation technics.

(417 words)

注：puppet　操り人形　The Adventures of Prince Achmed　アクメッド王子の冒険

(1) 下線部①と②の意味に最も近いものの組み合わせとして正しいものを選び，記号で答えなさい。

ア　① spread　② faced　　　　イ　① became famous　② respected

ウ　① died　② very interested　エ　① be successful　② fastened

（　　　）

(2) 下線部③を日本語になおしなさい。

_____

(3) 下線部④は具体的にどういうことかを日本語で説明しなさい。

_____

_____

(4) Reiniger がアニメーションの母と考えられる理由を2点，日本語で述べなさい。

1点目：_____

_____

2点目：_____

_____

(5) 本文の内容と一致するものを2つ選び，記号で答えなさい。

ア　Reiniger is famed as an animator in the animation industry.

イ　Reiniger had worked with the help of her friend.

ウ　Reiniger was given inspiration by the previous generation of animators.

エ　Reiniger developed a new type of technic, which the younger generation of animators used.

オ　It is unclear why Reiniger's works are becoming popular.

（　　　）

1 Choose the correct answer.

(1) The spring has (come / came), so cherry blossoms are blooming.

(2) People get some bonuses (in / on) addition to their monthly salary.

(3) Scientists are becoming (increasingly / increasing) aware of the problem.

(4) Her (popular / popularity) has declined since the scandal.

(5) The train (had / has) already left when I got to the station.

2 Fill in the blanks to complete the sentences.

(1) 脚を骨折しました。従って，ダンス大会には参加できません。

I broke my leg. (   ), I cannot attend the dance contest.

(2) 私たちは昨年その協会に加盟しました。

We joined the (   ) last year.

(3) この学校は 50 年前に設立されました。

This school was (   ) 50 years ago.

(4) グローバル化には長所も短所もあります。

(   ) has its advantages and disadvantages.

3 Reorder the words in brackets so that they can make sense.

(1) (move / car / to / slowly / the / begun / has) on the street.

_____

(2) She (math / for / is / hard / prepare / studying / to) the exam.

_____

(3) I know that (League / for / stands / Baseball / MLB / Major).

_____

(4) Being (the / career / been / has / most / professional / a soccer player / desired).

_____

4 Translate the Japanese into English.

(1) アメリカ社会は競争が激しすぎます。

_____

(2) それは私たちにとって重大な問題です。

_____

(3) 彼は有能な英語話者になりました。

_____

(4) 小さな健康習慣が人生に大きな違いをもたらします。

_____

1   Choose the correct answer.

(1) I have been (studying / studied) French for 5 years.

(2) Why would you like to work for an (overseas / oversea) company?

(3) He has sung (professional / professionally) with famous musicians.

(4) I cannot (call / recall) what we were talking then.

(5) The first language of many Brazilians is (Spanish / Portuguese).

2   Fill in the blanks to complete the sentences.

(1) イタリアにいる私の代理人に連絡してください。

Please contact my (　　　　　　) in Italy.

(2) かなりの数の者がそれに反対しました。

Quite (　　　　　) (　　　　　　) of people disagreed with it.

(3) 私はその言語に普遍的な特徴を見つけ，それが私の学習をより簡単にしました。

I found some universal features in the language, (　　　　　　) made my learning easier.

(4) この方法で，我々は長期的に競争性を保てるでしょう。

In this way, we can remain competitive in the (　　　　　) (　　　　　).

3   Reorder the words in brackets so that they can make sense.

(1) The soccer (of English / command / has / player / good / a).

_____

(2) He (three / abroad / soccer / in / played / professional / has / clubs).

_____

(3) Everyone loved John's video, (car / had / which / filmed / in / his / he).

_____

(4) They say that (success / to / a key / foreign / is / soccer / in / language / clubs).

_____

4   Translate the Japanese into English.

(1) 言葉によるコミュニケーションはそのとき必要ありませんでした。

_____

(2) 私の叔父は一流の会社で 10 年間働いています。

_____

(3) 私の母はロンドンに住んでいて，手紙を送ってくれました。

_____

(4) 地球は太陽の周りをまわっていて，惑星と呼ばれます。

_____

1 Choose the correct answer.

(1) The restaurant provides us with water without (charge / change).

(2) She is capable (of / on) using the computer.

(3) The school was (found / founded) in 1986.

(4) He has been (globally / global) known as a great actor.

(5) I aim to (improve / improving) my speaking skills.

2 Fill in the blanks to complete the sentences.

(1) 美の概念は時代とともに変わります。

The (   ) of beauty changes with the times.

(2) 関東は日本の主要大都市圏の一つです。

Kanto is a major (   ) area of Japan.

(3) 無私無欲の愛は存在すると思いますか。

Do you think (   ) love exists?

(4) あの会社は社員を育成しようとしていません。

That company is not trying to (   ) its employees.

3 Reorder the words in brackets so that they can make sense.

(1) I (aid / received / financial / any / from / never / have) the government.

_____

(2) We can (the / by / information / use / get / of / making / of / Internet / a lot).

_____

(3) (enter / endeavor / to / of / a / continuing / the purpose / is / my) good college.

_____

(4) He has (his / many / cultivated / skills / by / communication / people / meeting).

_____

4 Translate the Japanese into English.

(1) その会社は私たちに重要な情報を提供しました。

_____

(2) 私たちの支店の数は最大 200 まで増えました。

_____

(3) 東京に引っ越すまでこんな高い建物を見たことがありませんでした。

_____

(4) 彼らはユニセフ（UNICEF）を設立しました。それは貧しい子どもたちを助けています。

_____

1　Choose the correct answer.

(1)　Dogs are cute. (Moreover / More over), they are smart.

(2)　She was (active / actively) looking for a job.

(3)　It was cold (throughout / thought) the day.

(4)　You should negotiate (with / to) your agent.

(5)　I don't play any sports (rather than / other than) basketball.

2　Fill in the blanks to complete the sentences.

(1)　母の誕生日に香水をあげました。

I gave my mother (　　　　　　) for her birthday.

(2)　彼女は我が子の言語能力に驚かされました。

She was surprised by her child's (　　　　　) ability.

(3)　将来はスポーツ用具のデザインがしたいです。

I want to design sports (　　　　　) in the future.

(4)　MIT メディアラボはマサチューセッツ工科大学にある研究所です。

MIT Media (　　　　　) is a laboratory at the Massachusetts Institute of Technology.

3　Reorder the words in brackets so that they can make sense.

(1)　All the (common / reputable / something / companies / in / have).

_____

(2)　Kawashima Eiji is (who / only / the / athlete / not / skills / values / foreign language).

_____

(3)　Did (than /see / anyone / other / Kiyoshi) her?

_____

4　Translate the Japanese into English.

(1)　彼女の姉は神戸支店に配属されました。

_____

(2)　彼はクラスで一番のサッカー選手としてみなされています。

_____

(3)　私は次の世代を育成するサッカースクールに通っています。

_____

(4)　夢を実現させるために私は６年間ずっと一生懸命勉強をしています。

_____

1 Choose the correct word from ① to ④ to fill in the blank.

(1) He has (　　　　) in Fukuoka for ten years.

　　① lives　　　　② live　　　　③ living　　　　④ lived

(2) Kenji (　　　　) his homework for summer vacation yesterday.

　　① finished　　② finishes　　③ has finished　　④ have finished

(3) Kate (　　　　) Kyoto before she stayed in Tokyo.

　　① visits　　　② visited　　　③ had visited　　④ has visited

(4) My son has been reading a book (　　　　) this morning.

　　① in　　　　　② for　　　　③ on　　　　　④ since

(5) John said there had been no test in class, (　　　　) was a lie.

　　① that　　　　② which　　　③ who　　　　④ whose

2 Fill in the blanks to complete the sentences.

(1) トレーシーはここでどのくらいの期間，教師をしているのですか。

　　(　　　　　) (　　　　　) (　　　　　　) Tracey been a teacher here?

(2) 私は長い間，このチョコレートを試してみたいと思っています。

　　I (　　　　　) (　　　　　) to try this chocolate (　　　　　) a long time.

(3) 私たちは予想していたよりもお金を使いました。

　　We spent more money (　　　　　) we (　　　　　) (　　　　　).

(4) 昨日からずっとひどく雨が降っています。

　　It (　　　　　) (　　　　　) raining heavily (　　　　　) yesterday.

(5) 私の父が私にこの道具をくれましたが，それは父が10年前に買ったものでした。

　　My father gave me this tool, (　　　　　) he (　　　　　) (　　　　　) ten years ago.

(6) 私はちょうど駅に行ってきたところです。

　　I (　　　　　) (　　　　　) (　　　　　) to the station.

(7) カオリは1度だけ英語のネイティブスピーカーと話したことがあります。

　　Kaori (　　　　　) (　　　　　) with a native English speaker only (　　　　　).

(8) 私の父は看護師を30年間勤めて退職しました。

　　My father (　　　　　) (　　　　　) a nurse (　　　　　) 30 years before he retired.

(9) 私たちは北海道に1度も行ったことがありません。

　　We (　　　　　) (　　　　　) (　　　　　) to Hokkaido.

3 Reorder the words in brackets so that they can make sense.

(1) (gone / my daughter / to help / abroad / has) people in need.

_____

(2) She (not / told / Keita / me / arrived / yet / that / had).

_____

(3) (repairing / they / long / the copy machine / how / been / have)?

_____

(4) (been / regarding / there / global warming / have / many problems) recently.

_____

(5) (got to / left / the train / when / had / we / the station / already).

_____

(6) I got tired (for hours / she / been / because / taking me around / had).

_____

(7) (considered / to / three ways / the issue / have / solve / been) so far.

_____

(8) (Karen / many / you / times / heard from / how / have) in the past few years?

_____ in the past few years?

(9) I'm a fan of Mr. Murakami, (I / whose / reading / finished / new book) soon.

_____

(10) (the English lesson / have / signed up for / yet / you)?

_____

4 Translate the Japanese into English.

(1) 彼女は試験に失敗しましたが，それはめったにないことです。（めったにない＝ rarely）

She failed the exam, _____ .

(2) あなたは今までに海外で地下鉄に乗ったことがありますか。（乗る＝ take）

_____

(3) 私は彼女が話すまで離婚について1度も考えたことがありませんでした。（離婚＝ divorce）

_____ before she told about it.

(4) 私はオリンピックの試合を夜通し見ていました。（過去完了進行形で）

_____ Olympic Games all night.

(5) 私たちは子どもの時から知り合いです。（知り合いだ＝ know each other）

_____

(6) 彼女はそこで撮った写真を私に見せました。

She showed me the picture that _____ .

(7) ボブは新たな仕事に就きましたが，彼の友だちは皆知りません。

Bob found a new job, _____ .

Why is French Used at the Olympics?

In the summer of 2021, the Tokyo 2020 Olympic and Paralympic Games were finally held after (postpone) a year due to the pandemic. The Opening Ceremony took place at the National Stadium in Tokyo which was built for a maximum capacity of 68,000 spectators on July 23. Due to the pandemic, there was only a small crowd gathered
5　there. However, millions of people around the world could enjoy the ceremony on TV.

One tradition during the Opening Ceremony is the parade of nations. Team members from each (participate) country enter the stadium behind their national flags. For the Tokyo 2020 Games, 205 countries were represented and as each team entered the stadium, three announcements were made. The first one was in French, the second in
10　English and the third was in Japanese, the language of the host country. Though English is the most widely spoken language in the world, you might wonder ①(　　) French was used. The reason for this can be traced back to the first modern Olympic Games held in 1896.

The founder of the modern Olympics was Baron Pierre de Coubertin, a Frenchman.
15　He had always been interested in sports, especially the British system of sports in education. Originally, his goal was to bring similar sports education to French school children but eventually, his vision expanded beyond that to the dream of reviving the ancient Olympic games. ②(sports, make, was, that, world peace, he, the power, convinced, to, had).

20　He later founded the International Olympic Committee (IOC) and in 1896, the first modern Olympics ③were held in Greece (bring) 14 nations together. A total of 241 athletes competed in 43 events during the games.

An official document, called the Olympic Charter, was written by Coubertin around 1898 to clearly state the rules for holding future Olympic Games. In the document,
25　Article 23 states that all announcements should first be made in French, the official language of the Olympic Games, (follow) by English. The language of the host country would then follow.

There are a lot of traditions associated with the Olympic Games and the use of French is just one of them. The next time you hear the announcements, think about the
30　man who had the idea to bring the Olympics to the modern world, Pierre de Coubertin.

(382 words)

34

(1) （　　　　）内の語を正しい形に変えなさい。ただし，postpone は２語に，他は１語とする。

postpone → _____　　participate → _____

bring　　 → _____　　follow　　 → _____

(2) 下線部①の（　　　　）に入る関係詞を答えなさい。

_____

(3) Baron Pierre de Coubertin の最初の目標とその後の夢が何であったかを日本語で説明しなさい。

最初の目標：_____

その後の夢：_____

(4) 下線部②が「彼はスポーツには世界平和を成す力があることを確信していた」という意味の英文になるように，（　　）内の語句を並べ替えなさい。

_____

(5) 下線部③と同じ意味となる語句を文中から探し，２語で答えなさい。

_____

(6) 本文の内容と一致するものを２つ選び，記号で答えなさい。

ア　The language used at the last announcement in the Opening Ceremony of the Olympics changes each time.

イ　Each athlete taking part in the events entered the stadium in the Opening Ceremony of the Olympics, regardless of her or his nationality.

ウ　IOC was established after the first modern Olympics.

エ　The rule about the announcements in the Opening Ceremony of the Olympics is prescribed in a document.

オ　The rules about the Olympics are just traditions and are not specified in writing.

（　　　　　　）

1 Choose the correct answer.

(1) Although she was (untrained / trained), she was skillful in art.

(2) They work for physically (challenging / challenged) people.

(3) You should be (mental / mentally) prepared for it.

(4) He was killed at home, but no one else was there. Thus, I think an (insider / outsider)
     killed him.

2 Fill in the blanks to complete the sentences.

(1) 多数の日本人が海外に住んでいます。

     (   ) (   ) (   ) (   ) Japanese people live overseas.

(2) 私の父はスポーツ愛好家です。

     My father is a sports (   ).

(3) 政府からの経済的援助が期待できません。

     Financial aid from the government cannot (   ) (   ).

(4) まず, その絵には様々な色が使われています。

     To start with, there are various colors in the (   ).

3 Reorder the words in brackets so that they can make sense.

(1) (put / if / some / you / music / on / can) you like.

     _____

(2) The value of *art brut* (in / powerful / lies / expressions / simple / its / but).

     _____

(3) I like the museum, (works / inside / beautiful / exhibits / which / glass).

     _____

(4) (cars / will / display / sale / they / foreign / for) next week.

     _____

4 Translate the Japanese into English.

(1) 日本の皇室の一人を見たことがあります。

     _____

(2) 彼女の鉛筆画は外国人に人気があります。

     _____

(3) 美術館とは美術展が見られる場所です。

     _____

(4) そのパンは障がい者の方によって作られているかもしれません。

     _____

1 Choose the correct answer.

(1) Your job is to help people with (abilities / disabilities).

(2) You should use (informal / formal) language to your teachers.

(3) To everyone's (surprise / surprising), her English was perfect.

(4) That is the house (which / where) we lived before.

2 Fill in the blanks to complete the sentences.

(1) 彼は優秀な学生です。

He is an (   ) student.

(2) 京都は外国人に人気の都市ですが，奈良もです。

Kyoto is a popular city among foreigners, but Nara (   ) (   ).

(3) 私は夫と 30 年前に初めて出会いました。

I first met my husband three (   ) ago.

(4) 彼女は毎日 8 時間勉強しました。そのようにして彼女は入試に受かりました。

She studied 8 hours every day. This is (   ) she passed the entrance exam.

3 Reorder the words in brackets so that they can make sense.

(1) Unfortunately, (receive / them / education / of / could / proper / none).

_____

(2) We visited (with / special / institution / children / the / needs / where) lived.

_____

(3) (take / the day / is / piano / Thursday / I / a / when) lesson.

_____

(4) With or without physical challenges, (education / should / right / everyone / a / have / to).

_____

4 Translate the Japanese into English.

(1) その歌手は昨年 2 つの賞を受賞しました。

_____

(2) 彼女の役者としてのデビューは 1992 年でした。

_____

(3) 私は高等教育機関で勤めています。

_____

(4) 障がいがあろうとなかろうと，私たちはみんな人権を持っています。

_____

1 Choose the correct answer.

(1) I will engage (in / at) the club activities more from tomorrow.

(2) There are a (various / variety) of opinions about the origin of Japanese Udon.

(3) He is a New York Yankees (supporter / support).

(4) I am interested in making (documentary / document) movies.

(5) We are still cleaning. (In / On) the meantime, you can drink some coffee there.

2 Fill in the blanks to complete the sentences.

(1) タカはそのイベントに参加する予定です。

Taka is going to (   ) in the event.

(2) 彼らは年に一度文化祭を開催します。

They hold a school festival (   ).

(3) 特別食の要望にはお応えします。

We will (   ) requests for special meals.

(4) 虹の中には７つの違いがはっきりした色があると日本では言います。

People say a rainbow has seven (   ) colors in it in Japan.

3 Reorder the words in brackets so that they can make sense.

(1) (was / when / tired / on / felt / I / working / I) the weekend.

_____

(2) I (invited / would / thought / to / earnestly / we / be) the party.

_____

(3) We (argument / problem / monetary / an / had / about / a).

_____

(4) (to / outside / Aki / attempt / not / go / did) yesterday because of the rain.

_____

4 Translate the Japanese into English.

(1) 社会福祉について考えてみましょう。

_____

(2) この会社は様々な製品を作っています。

_____

(3) メールに添付されている写真を確認してください。

_____

(4) その機関に入学するための必要条件は何ですか。

_____

1   Choose the correct answer.

(1) Higher education comes after (primary / secondary) education.

(2) They built some (facilities / equipment) for the Tokyo Olympics.

(3) Olivia works for a (childcare / childrencare) center.

(4) That coffee shop is run by (disabling / disabled) people.

(5) Our parents celebrate their wedding (annually / anniversary) once a year.

2   Fill in the blanks to complete the sentences.

(1) その協会の設立は多くの企業に支援されました。

The (   ) of the association was supported by many companies.

(2) その国の独立は毎年多くの人に祝われます。

The (   ) of the country is celebrated by many people every year.

(3) 仕事に対する長期の献身が日本では求められます。

A long-term (   ) to the job is required in Japan.

(4) 統合された市場として，ヨーロッパは世界でより重要になりつつあります。

As an (   ) market, Europe is becoming more important in the world.

3   Reorder the words in brackets so that they can make sense.

(1) The teacher (importance / the / taught / self-reliance / of / us).

_____

(2) We should (support / to / welfare / raise / for / weak people / money).

_____

(3) (for / is / people / active / caring / still / those / she / in) though she is over 90 years old.

_____

(4) It (home / a / as / private / started / small / care) for elderly people.

_____

4   Translate the Japanese into English.

(1) その建物の設立者は私の祖父です。

_____

(2) この仕事は明日までに終わるはずです。

_____

(3) 20 世紀を振り返る雑誌がたくさんあります。

_____

(4) 金銭的なトラブルによりその学校を運営するのが難しくなりました。

_____

1 Choose the correct word from ① to ④ to fill in the blank.

(1) This computer (   ) in the morning.

　　① can use　　② can used　　③ cannot be used　④ cannot use

(2) Is that the reason (   ) you were late for work?

　　① when　　② why　　③ how　　④ which

(3) They kept (   ) around the clock.

　　① worked　② be working　③ being worked　④ working

(4) A decision (   ) right now.

　　① must make　② must be made　③ make　④ made

(5) He was born on the day (   ) it snowed heavily.

　　① when　② where　③ which　④ why

2 Fill in the blanks to complete the sentences.

(1) その業務は明日までに終わらせるべきです。

　　The assignment (   ) (   ) (   ) by tomorrow.

(2) これが私たちが心配しているただ１つの点です。

　　This is only the (   ) (   ) we are worried about.

(3) 私たちは学校の屋上で空を見上げながら立っていました。

　　We were (   ) (   ) up at the sky on the roof of our school.

(4) そのようにして私の日本での新しい生活が始まりました。

　　(   ) (   ) (   ) my new life in Japan began.

(5) 彼女はその親近感で皆に愛されるに違いありません。

　　She (   ) (   ) (   ) by everyone because of her friendliness.

(6) オリンピックが開かれる年は 2021 年に変更されました。

　　The (   ) (   ) the Olympics will be held was changed to 2021.

(7) 交換は遅くとも金曜日までに完了するでしょう。

　　The replacement (   ) (   ) (   ) by Friday at the latest.

(8) 彼がどうやって危険から逃れたかは謎です。

　　(   ) he escaped from danger is a mystery.

(9) 彼女はお気に入りのお店が閉店するという知らせを聞いて驚いたように見えました。

　　She (   ) (   ) at the news that her favorite shop would close.

3 Reorder the words in brackets so that they can make sense.

(1) You (the whole stage / you / from / can / sitting / where / are / see).

_____

(2) I (came home / how / don't / I / from far away / remember).

_____

(3) (not / must / be / during the lecture / your mobile phone / used).

_____

(4) I don't understand (to / why / with SNS / hurt / so many people / try / others).

_____

(5) (feel / us / exhausted / makes / this summer heat).

_____

(6) (any places / park / where / are / can / our cars / there / we)?

_____

(7) (seen / can / be / here / many stars) in the evening?

_____

(8) (most of us / the night / when / go to bed / is).

_____

(9) We (got / become / has / that / lost / have / he / worried) on his way here.

_____

(10) I talked to a little boy (he / alone / sat / since / crying) on a bench.

_____

4 Translate the Japanese into English.

(1) 私は自分の経験を活かせる仕事に就きたいです。(where を使って，活かす = use)
   I want a job _____ .

(2) 私が電話をかけている理由は製品の値段を確認するためです。(why を使って)
   _____ is to confirm the prize of the product.

(3) 大きな書店で探せば，その雑誌は見つかるはずです。(受動態で)
   _____ if you look for it in a large bookstore.

(4) その事故で誰もけがをしませんでした。
   Nobody _____ .

(5) あなたが後悔する時が来るでしょう。
   _____ you will regret it.

(6) 参加者が10人未満であれば，そのイベントは中止されるかもしれません。(受動態で)
   _____ if fewer than 10 persons take part in it.

(7) その機械がどのように作動するかをお見せしましょう。
   I'll _____ .

41

High School Memories in the US

The last time I visited the US, I dropped by my old high school. It felt strange to be back in the school's halls again after so many years. As I walked around, a flood of memories came over me and I asked myself "Did you enjoy high school?" I had to think hard about the answer, but in the end, I realized that while there were ①challenging times, I also had many great memories.

One of the most enjoyable weeks of the school year was ②Homecoming Week. It was called this because at the end of that week, a football game was scheduled on the school's home field. To get students excited for it, the week before was designated "Spirit Week" and each day had a different theme. For example, one day was "wear a silly hat day" and another was "dress like a cowboy day." On a game day, all the students gathered in the gymnasium for a performance by the cheerleaders. The day after, there was a casual dance held at the gymnasium (A   ) a DJ was hired to play music, or a local band played live.

Another big event during the year was the formal dance party held each spring, called prom. It was a very big deal, and everyone thought a lot about (B   ) to invite as a date. Dressing up in formal wear for the first time was so much fun. Boys rented fancy tuxedos and girls bought colorful formal dresses to wear. Many students hired limousines for the evening and some hosted parties at their homes afterwards.

Of course, ③American high school was not all fun. There was a lot of pressure especially during the last two years when it was important to maintain good grades. It was a challenge to balance my school life with my part-time job. In addition, applying to colleges was stressful because it took a lot of work to write long essays about personal experiences and ambitions for the future.

I was glad I took the time to visit my high school after so long. ④It (appreciate, there, me, to, the experiences, a chance, I had, gave) and to realize how much I had changed since then. I'll definitely be back again in a few years.

(378 words)

注：prom　（高校などの）卒業記念のダンスパーティー

42

(1) 下線部①に最も近い意味の語を1つ選び，記号で答えなさい。

ア　hard　　　イ　favorable　　ウ　hesitating　　エ　unrealistic

（　　　）

(2) 下線部②のように呼ばれる週がある理由を示す次の文の空欄を補い，文を完成させなさい。

週の終わりに，（　　　　　　　　　　　　　　　　　　　　　　　　）予定が組まれ，それまでの1週間，日々さまざまな（　　　　　　　　　）で催しが行われる週だから。

(3) （　A　），（　B　）に入る語として正しいものを1つずつ選び，記号で答えなさい。

ア　how　　　　イ　who　　　ウ　which　　　エ　what　　　オ　where

A（　　　）　B（　　　）

(4) 下線部③の例として正しくないものを1つ選び，記号で答えなさい。

ア　Students had to take much effort to prepare to enter universities.

イ　It was difficult for students to decide how much time they should spare for activities outside school.

ウ　All the students were required to join the practice of football throughout the year.

エ　There was a period in which students had to continue giving good results at school.

（　　　）

(5) 下線部④が意味が通る英文となるように，（　　　）内の語句を並べかえなさい。

_____

(6) 本文の内容と一致するものを1つ選び，記号で答えなさい。

ア　Every time the author went to the US, the author visited her or his old high school.

イ　The students of the author's old high school were wearing the same clothes throughout the "Spirit week."

ウ　The high school the author attended had a party in spring, and then the students were absorbed in their clothes.

エ　The author is thinking of visiting her or his old high school after many years.

（　　　）

1 Choose the correct answer.

(1) A large number of people participated (at / in) the local event.

(2) She said, "We can do it by (ourself / ourselves)."

(3) In New York, as (in / if) most big cities, you can see many tall buildings.

(4) Since the car ahead of me was too slow, I changed (lanes / lines).

2 Fill in the blanks to complete the sentences.

(1) 交通渋滞につかまっていました。

I was caught in a traffic (   ).

(2) どんな乗り物を運転できますか。

What kind of (   ) can you drive?

(3) 保育士の不足は大きな社会問題です。

A (   ) of childcare workers is a big social problem.

(4) ミキはピアノを上手に弾きます。その上，歌も上手です。

Miki plays the piano well. (   ) (   ), she is a good singer as well.

3 Reorder the words in brackets so that they can make sense.

(1) I heard that its (can / function / chat / useful / video / be).

_____

(2) (eat / allow / our mother / to / will / us) a lot of junk food?

_____

(3) There (three languages / speak / are / can / who / those) in the world.

_____

(4) Should I press (button / coffee / the auto / maker / the / on)?

_____

4 Translate the Japanese into English.

(1) 自動運転車を持っている人を誰か知っていますか。

_____

(2) あなたにあの顧客を対処していただきたいです。

_____

(3) 今日の夕方は夕食の準備で忙しいです。

_____

(4) その新しい技術は交通事故を減らすだろうと言われています。

_____

1 Choose the correct answer.

(1) Let's (image / imagine). You have won a million dollars.

(2) I couldn't see the (oncoming / incoming) cars behind.

(3) You must turn right here immediately, or you'll (crush / crash).

(4) What (about / if) the train is late?

2 Fill in the blanks to complete the sentences.

(1) 下道の代わりに高速道路に乗りましょう。

Let's take the (　　　　　　) instead of the local road.

(2) 私はベッドの端で寝るのが好きです。

I like to sleep on the (　　　　　　) of a bed.

(3) 私の友人は優秀なプログラマーです。

My friend is an outstanding (　　　　　　).

(4) 崖から落ちないように気をつけてください。

Be careful to not fall off the (　　　　　　).

3 Reorder the words in brackets so that they can make sense.

(1) We can see (side / on / ocean / the / left / the).

_____

(2) (lane / go / if / the opposite / you / into), you will hit the car.

_____

(3) (down / were / the street / traveling / we) in a self-driving car.

_____

(4) (decision / make / a / you / need to / quick) right now.

4 Translate the Japanese into English.

(1) 真っ直ぐ行ってから右に曲がってください。

_____

(2) もし私がお金持ちなら，ロサンゼルスに住めるのに。

_____

(3) 交通事故が起きて，私は道路に投げ出されました。

_____

(4) ここで左に曲がることは多くの人を殺めることを意味します。

_____

1　Choose the correct answer.

(1)　The doors can move (automatically / automatic).

(2)　There is a (possibly / possibility) that I will win the award.

(3)　"Magic sugar." This (may / may not) sound good, but, in fact, it's not healthy.

(4)　The (criminal / crime) escaped from the police station.

2　Fill in the blanks to complete the sentences.

(1)　かかわってくるリスクには注意します。

　　　I will be careful about the risks (　　　　　　　).

(2)　緊急事態のため，外出してはいけません。

　　　Because of the state of (　　　　　　　), you must not go out.

(3)　人を傷つけることはどんな状況においても正当化されるべきではありません。

　　　Hurting people shouldn't be (　　　　　　　) in any situation.

(4)　早期に発見すれば，癌は命にかかわる病ではありません。

　　　If found at an early stage, cancer is not a (　　　　　　　) disease.

3　Reorder the words in brackets so that they can make sense.

(1)　Sadly, (over / a kangaroo / on / a truck / the road / ran).

　　　_____

(2)　You should (circumstances / harm / any / not / the environment / under).

　　　_____

(3)　There is (of / by / getting / a car / a chance / hit) if you ever go out.

　　　_____

(4)　What if the cars (are / those who / avoid / walking / to / are programmed)?

　　　_____

4　Translate the Japanese into English.

(1)　彼の話は真実であるはずがありません。

　　　_____

(2)　タカは交通事故に巻き込まれました。

　　　_____

(3)　彼らは犯罪者としてみなされています。

　　　_____

(4)　もし 100 万円持っていたら，何を買いますか。

　　　_____

1   Correct the word to complete the sentence.

(1) She was busy (practice) the guitar.   _____

(2) What would you do if you (be) a programmer?   _____

(3) He often tells a lie, so this (can) be true.   _____

(4) I (hope) I could touch the stars in the sky.   _____

2   Fill in the blanks to complete the sentence that matches the following in meaning.

(1) We have decided on what we must do as a team.

   = We have (   ) a (   ) on what we must do as a team.

(2) Those who don't use their smartphones are rare.

   = (   ) who don't use their smartphones are rare.

(3) She hit someone with her car when driving at night.

   = She (   ) (   ) someone when driving at night.

(4) My father let me play the violin at home when I was a child.

   = My father (   ) me (   ) play the violin at home when I was a child.

(5) He is smart. Moreover, he has a variety of hobbies.

   = He is smart. (   ) (   ), he has a variety of hobbies.

3   Translate English into the Japanese.

(1) The teacher advised us not to look at the textbook.

_____

(2) You may find it difficult to drive on the highway.

_____

(3) My mother left home before 8 a.m., so she should be at work by now.

_____

(4) What if you miss a turn and fall off the cliff?

_____

(5) How would you justify the argument if you were him?

_____

1　Choose the correct word from ① to ④ to fill in the blank.

(1)　If you see Helen, please ask her (　　　) my office.

　　① stops by　　② stopped by　　③ stop by　　④ to stop by

(2)　If I had enough time, I (　　　) go out with her.

　　① could be　　② could　　③ can　　④ can be

(3)　He (　　　) us to do the job soon.

　　① enabled　　② prevented　　③ kept　　④ made

2　Fill in the blanks to complete the sentences.

(1)　そんな時間に彼女がそこにいるはずがありません。

　　She (　　　　) (　　　　) there at that hour.

(2)　担当医は私に砂糖を使いすぎないように助言しました。

　　My physician (　　　　) me (　　　　) (　　　　) use too much sugar.

(3)　重労働で私たちは疲れ果てました。

　　The hard work (　　　　) us (　　　　) (　　　　) exhausted.

(4)　私があなたの立場にいるなら，プロジェクトを休止するでしょう。（仮定法過去）

　　If I (　　　　) in your position, I (　　　　) suspend the project.

(5)　台風の影響でお祭りは中止せざるを得ないでしょう。

　　We will (　　　　) (　　　　) (　　　　) cancel the festival due to the typhoon.

(6)　この文書は私たちに定期的に室温を確認することを念押しするものです。

　　This document (　　　　) us (　　　　) (　　　　) the room temperature regularly.

(7)　雨が降っていなければ，もっと多くの人がピクニックに参加するはずです。（仮定法過去）

　　If it (　　　　) (　　　　) (　　　　), more people (　　　　) participate in the picnic.

(8)　誰でもミスを起こし得ます。

　　Anybody (　　　　) (　　　　) mistakes.

(9)　私たちは学校に携帯電話を持ってくるのを認められていません。

　　We are (　　　　) (　　　　) (　　　　) bring our cellphones to school.

(10)　彼女みたいに英語が話せたらいいのに。

　　I (　　　　) (　　　　) (　　　　) speak English like her.

(11)　その標識はその地点で道路を横切らないように警告するものです。

　　The sign (　　　　) us (　　　　) (　　　　) cross the road at that point.

48

3 Reorder the words in brackets so that they can make sense.

(1) (fill out / to / are / the participants / the application form / required).

_____

(2) I (you / me / appreciate it / could / if / some information / would / give).

_____

(3) She is a boss (to / by themselves / allows / decide things / her staff members / who).

_____

(4) You (sleep well / if / might / you / feel better / could).

_____

(5) It (difficult / our life / shouldn't / imagine / without mobile phones / be / to).

_____

(6) (to be / persuade / of / our development team / her / shall we / a member)?

_____

(7) What (if / the offer / would / take / to us / didn't / we / happen)?

_____

(8) I'm (that / a cold / I / catch / may / afraid).

_____

(9) It's (children / to / have / encourage / to / a lot of experiences / important).

_____

(10) How (you / had / if / would / your days / enough time and money / you / spend)?

_____

(11) We (to / our company / the plan / reconsider / urged).

_____

4 Translate the Japanese into English.

(1) 寒いなら，暖房機をつけましょうか。(暖房機 = heater)

Do you want _____ if you feel cold?

(2) その住人にそこにゴミを捨てないように言ってもらえますか。(住人 = resident)

Would you _____ throw away garbage there?

(3) あなたが私なら，どんな PC を買いますか。(仮定法過去)

What PC _____ ?

(4) 今日，仕事に行く必要がなければいいのに。

_____

(5) 彼女は 1 時間でオフィスに到着するはずです。

_____

(6) ジェーンは彼女がどこにいるか知っているに違いないです。

_____

What Makes a Great Workplace?

What do you want to be when you grow up? When you were in elementary school, how did you answer this question? Did you want to be a professional athlete or work at a flower shop or bakery? ①By the time you graduate from high school or university, your job aspirations may change a lot. Choosing a job involves thinking about many things like salary and working

5　hours, but recent job-hunters also consider the workplace environment when deciding on a job.

In this respect, tech companies have focused a lot on ②(　　　). They try to create workplaces that are fun and comfortable to work in.

The tech giant Google, for example, is known for its workplace culture. Their philosophy is that if employees are happier, they will be more productive and stay with the company longer.

10　It's ③a win-win situation. That's why Google office environments are created with employee satisfaction in mind.

Employees working at the Google headquarters in the US, often called Googlers, generally don't have to leave during working hours because a lot of services are provided for them for free. Employees can enjoy any of the several cafes and restaurants within the company

15　buildings. Not only does ④this save time, but it's easier for them to interact with one another during the day.

If a Googler didn't have time to see the dentist for a teeth cleaning, there is an onsite dental office where they can get an appointment. If an employee didn't manage to get a haircut over the weekend, it's not a problem as the Google headquarters has a full-service salon. If an

20　employee has stiff shoulders from working at the computer too long, there's a massage service available.

In addition to such services, employee relaxation is also a priority. Employees in need of a break can find specially designed sleeping pods in which to take a nap, play a game of table tennis or try out the latest video games. There is even a fitness center and swimming pool

25　where they can exercise.

And it's not just Google that is creating these kinds of workplaces. Other tech companies like Facebook, Netflix and Amazon have also invested in improving their workplace environments. As companies compete for the best employees, the workplace environment is becoming an important consideration for job-hunters.

(389 words)

注：sleeping pod　スリープポッド（コンパクトなベッド等を備えた小さなスペース）

(1) 下線部①の理由として，就職希望者が職場環境以外に考慮することを2つ，日本語で答えなさい。

1つ目：＿＿＿＿＿＿＿＿　　　2つ目：＿＿＿＿＿＿＿＿

(2) 下線部②の（　　）内に最も適するものをア〜ウから1つ選び，記号で答えなさい。
ア　making more job-hunters decide to enter them
イ　making employees create their unique workplace environment
ウ　making workplace environments appealing to employees

（　　　　）

(3) 下線部③とはどういう状況かを日本語で具体的に説明しなさい。

＿＿＿＿＿＿＿＿＿＿＿＿＿＿＿＿＿＿＿＿＿＿＿＿＿＿＿＿＿＿＿＿＿＿＿＿＿

＿＿＿＿＿＿＿＿＿＿＿＿＿＿＿＿＿＿＿＿＿＿＿＿＿＿＿＿＿＿＿＿＿＿＿＿＿

(4) 下線部④を具体的に説明する次の文の空欄を補い，文を完成させなさい。
グーグル本社の従業員が（　　　　　　　　　　）中に（　　　　　　　　　　　）必要
がないこと。

(5) 本文の内容と一致するものを2つ選び，記号で答えなさい。
ア　Employees at the Google headquarters try to use facilities within the company buildings outside of working hours.
イ　Googlers have to pay for some of the services the Google headquarters provide.
ウ　Googlers cannot get medical care within the company buildings.
エ　The Google headquarters provide the services for employees who are exhausted by their hard work.
オ　There are still few companies that spend money on making better workplace environments.
カ　Job applicants should take the workplace environment into account.

（　　　　　　　　）

1 Choose the correct answer.

(1) We took (preparatory / prepare) courses before college.

(2) He was a (naturalist / natural) as well as a researcher of plants.

(3) My uncle is a famous (scholar / scholarship) in a certain field.

(4) I don't listen to any music other than (classics / traditions).

(5) Oda Nobunaga is a (historic / historical) person in Japan.

2 Fill in the blanks to complete the sentences.

(1) その本を書くのに様々な参考文献を読みました。

I read a wide variety of (　　　　　　　) works to write the book.

(2) 大都市圏では野生動物を見ることはないでしょう。

You'll never see any (　　　　　　　) in metropolitan areas.

(3) それらの標本を見て驚きました。

I was surprised to see those (　　　　　　　).

(4) テーブルの上にあるのは私のピザです。

(　　　　) (　　　　) (　　　　　　) is my pizza.

3 Reorder the words in brackets so that they can make sense.

(1) (made / America / fifty / up / of / is) states.

_____

(2) In order to make good soup, (by / milk / bit / you / add / should / bit).

_____

(3) (her / Joe / classmates / among / were) and Sam.

_____

(4) Cuba (where / born / I / is / the country / was).

_____

4 Translate the Japanese into English.

(1) 私もコーヒーが好きではありません。

_____

(2) 学生の頃，暗記するのは苦手でした。

_____

(3) 江戸時代に書かれた本を読みました。

_____

(4) 彼女は農業大学を今年卒業します。

_____

1　Choose the correct answer.

(1) He could get a (scholarship / relationship) from the institution.

(2) The (religion / religious) group has begun to be more active.

(3) I often read some academic (magazines / journals) for work.

(4) My (faithful / faith) lies in God.

(5) My favorite subject was (biology / history) because I liked animals and plants.

2　Fill in the blanks to complete the sentences.

(1) 彼らの素行不良を受け入れることはできません。

We cannot accept their bad (　　　　　　).

(2) 彼女の知性が彼女を京都大学へ導きました。

Her (　　　　　　) led her to Kyoto University.

(3) 彼らは多くのお金を障がい者のための学校に寄付しました。

They (　　　　　　) plenty of money to schools for people with disabilities.

(4) 彼は世界に変化をもたらした革命家の一人でした。

He was one of the (　　　　　　) who made a difference in the world.

3　Reorder the words in brackets so that they can make sense.

(1) Taka is (nature / boy / very / by / a / quiet).

_____

(2) (enthusiasm / changed / his / baseball / has / for) his career.

_____

(3) I want to learn (including / Greek / foreign languages, / Latin / and).

_____

(4) She is short-tempered, so (this / her temper / may / over / lose / she).

_____

4　Translate the Japanese into English.

(1) 臨時の仕事を見つけました。

_____

(2) 彼の好奇心が彼をこの学校に連れてきました。

_____

(3) 私の会社での功績は多くの注目を集めました。

_____

(4) その博物館は100万作品以上の手芸品を展示しています。

_____

1 Choose the correct answer.

(1) I found a (fungi / fungus) under the bed.

(2) We will (object to / object) their suggestion.

(3) Her (writing / writings) were popular among young readers.

(4) The party was (poorly / poor) organized.

(5) I must write this email (informally / formally) to the company for an interview.

2 Fill in the blanks to complete the sentences.

(1) 彼はロード・オブ・ザ・リングの著者です。

He is the (   ) of *The Lord of the Rings*.

(2) 嵐は徐々に弱まると思います。

I think the storm will (   ) bit by bit.

(3) 彼らは会社の方針は正しかったと主張しています。

They (   ) that their company's policy was right.

(4) 適切な政策があってこそ，政府は機能します。

With (   ) policies, the government can function.

3 Reorder the words in brackets so that they can make sense.

(1) She (of / the result / to / contributed / research / her) the magazine.

_____

(2) (seems / that thing / there / be / over / to) a slime mold.

_____

(3) (the nature / creatures / have / of / single-celled) plants and animals.

_____

(4) My (decision / to / concern / make / was / a) in the difficult situation.

_____

4 Translate the Japanese into English.

(1) ケンは彼の祖父にちなんで名付けられました。

_____

(2) あなたが警察に逮捕されて欲しくはありません。

_____

(3) 社会に貢献できる人間になりたいです。

_____

(4) 我々は２つの異なる宗教を結びつけることを目指しています。

_____

1   Choose the correct answer.

(1)   Her story was (inspiring / inspired) to me.

(2)   (Despite of / Despite) his achievements, he was not famous at all.

(3)   The weather is great, but (surprising / surprisingly), it will rain this afternoon.

(4)   (Ecology / Economy) is the study of relationships between creatures and the environment.

2   Fill in the blanks to complete the sentences.

(1)   私の友だちのお父さんは環境省に勤めています。

     My friend's father works for the (　　　　　　) of the Environment.

(2)   日本の天皇は国の象徴としてみなされています。

     The (　　　　　　) of Japan is considered as the symbol of the country.

(3)   彼の家族は動物保護団体に属しています。

     His family belongs to an animal (　　　　　　) group.

(4)   古い写真を見ると，私の栄光の日々をしばしば思い出します。

     When I see old photos of me, I often recall my (　　　　　　) days.

3   Reorder the words in brackets so that they can make sense.

(1)   The college (on / lectures / offers / free / plants).

     _____

(2)   She presented (slime / of / a / specimen / mold).

     _____

(3)   Minakata (in / them / put / old / boxes / candy).

     _____

(4)   He works (the / reserve / at / wildlife / the island / on).

     _____

4   Translate the Japanese into English.

(1)   私は旧友を認識できませんでした。

     _____

(2)   この岩は県の天然記念物です。

     _____

(3)   名声に加えて，彼は名誉をも手にしました。

     _____

(4)   その良い知らせは私たちを幸せにしました。

     _____

1 Follow the instructions and rewrite the following sentences.

(1) The swimmer jumped into the pool. (Into で始まる文に)

_____

(2) Kenta comes here. He will welcome you. (下線部を here で始まる文に)

_____ , who will welcome you.

(3) Kate seems to have a good time dancing. (It で始まる文に)

_____

(4) It doesn't seem that the book is written in English. (The book で始まる文に)

_____

(5) She seems to have forgotten my name. (It で始まる文に)

_____

2 Fill in the blanks to complete the sentences.

(1) あなたの手助けのおかげで，私たちは時間に間に合って仕事を終えることができました。

Your help (   ) us (   ) complete the task in time.

(2) 彼女の心温まる手紙で私たちは幸せな気分になりました。

Her heart-warming letter (   ) us feel happy.

(3) この学校の中心に大きな木があります。

(   ) the (   ) of this school (   ) a big tree.

(4) 彼らはその結果に不満であるように思えました。

(   ) (   ) that they (   ) unhappy with the result.

(5) 彼のプレゼントにカレンは喜びました。

His present (   ) Karen.

(6) 私たちは彼の態度に驚きませんでした。

His attitude (   ) (   ) us.

(7) この道路の下に地下鉄が走っています。

(   ) this road (   ) the subway.

(8) 彼女は上司とうまくいっていないようです。

She (   ) (   ) (   ) get along with her boss.

(9) 彼は不断の努力により出版業界で成功しました。

His constant effort (   ) (   ) his success in the publishing industry.

(10) この本を読んで，私はいい考えが浮かびました。

This book (   ) me a good idea.

56

3 Reorder the words in brackets so that they can make sense.

(1) (prevented / starting / them / what / from / their business) smoothly?

_____

(2) (had / that / it / the two researchers / seem / the same opinions / didn't).

_____

(3) (will / you / minutes' / from here / bring / the city hall / walk / a few / to).

_____

(4) Right (is / the corner / the library / around).

_____

(5) (of / that picture / me / reminds / the day) I met her for the first time.

_____

(6) (easy / to / made / this handout / the students / it / the class / for / understand).

_____

(7) (have no choice / rely on / to / seem / but / him / we / to).

_____

(8) On (with / stood / flowers / his mother / his left).

_____

(9) (show / didn't / the news / whether / us) there were injured people in the accident.

_____

(10) (keep up with / to / don't / be able to / we / the pace / seem).

_____

4 Translate the Japanese into English.

(1) 嵐が原因でバスの運行に遅れが生じました。(The storm を主語に)

_____ in the bus service.

(2) 私はあなたのテキストをなくしてしまったようです。

I _____ .

(3) 部屋から1人の少年が青ざめた顔をして慌てて出てきました。(慌てて出てくる = rush out)

Out of _____ looking pale.

(4) 彼は正直であるため，うそをつけません。(allow を使って)

His honesty _____ .

(5) 彼は電車に間に合うために急いでいるようです。(It で始めて，急いで = in a hurry)

_____

(6) なぜ彼は突然，仕事を辞めたのですか。(what を使って)

_____

(7) そのニュースは誤りであったようです。

The news _____ .

Boracay Island and Overtourism

Boracay is a small island in the Philippines with a total land area of 10.32 square km. The island is only 7 km long and at its narrowest point under 1 km wide. Beginning in the 1970s, Boracay gradually became a popular destination as tourists were drawn to its tranquil turquoise waters and white sand beaches. Unfortunately, in 2018, the island that

5　had once been called "a paradise on earth" was shut to tourists after enduring decades of environmental damage.

The number of tourists traveling to Boracay steadily increased throughout the 1980s. Later, when luxury hotels started opening, the number jumped from 260,000 in 2000 to 650,000 in 2009. In 2012, it was awarded "Best Island" by a famous travel magazine

10　and experienced an increase in tourist arrivals, receiving 1.2 million that year. By 2017, with more than 2 million visitors, the island's beauty was nearly completely destroyed because of too many tourists. This is called ①overtourism.

Too many visitors, ②a poor infrastructure and the government's failure to enforce laws turned Boracay into an environmental disaster area. The lack of sewage and waste

15　treatment facilities caused serious health problems. For instance, the most popular beaches on Boracay had terrible water pollution that caused skin infections and stomach problems. In addition, unmonitored snorkeling and illegal fishing destroyed about 70 percent of the island's coral reefs.

In 2018, the President of the Philippines, Rodrigo Duterte, declared an environmental

20　emergency on the island and closed it for the next six months. During that time, work was completed to rehabilitate the island. A new efficient sewage treatment system was built, and a plan was developed to ensure sustainable tourism for the future.

Once the island opened, ③several new policies were introduced. Most importantly, the number of tourists allowed to enter each day was limited to 6,405. ④Those arriving were

25　also required to show hotel reservations to prove they were staying at a registered hotel. Single-use plastic was completely prohibited.

Overtourism is a major issue for many tourist destinations around the world. Hopefully, governments will reconsider the tourism model that "the more tourism, the better" and develop policies to ensure a sustainable future so that we can continue to

30　enjoy tourist spots while protecting their natural beauty.　　　　　　　(372 words)

注：turquoise　青緑色の

(1) ボラカイ島における下線部①の状況について，日本語で説明しなさい。

_____

_____

(2) 下線部②とほぼ同じ意味の表現を本文から英語のまま書き抜きなさい。

_____

(3) 下線部③の具体例を日本語で答えなさい。

_____

(4) 下線部④を日本語になおしなさい。ただし，"Those arriving"の部分を具体的に述べること。

_____

_____

(5) 本文の内容と一致するものを2つ選び，記号で答えなさい。

ア　The beauty in Boracay was revealed by the development of the island.

イ　Too many visitors to Boracay directly influenced the health of the residents of the island.

ウ　Some activities did harm to the marine environment around Boracay.

エ　There was a period when tourists could not enter Boracay.

オ　Some nations think it impossible to balance prosperous tourist destinations and protecting the environment.

（　　　　　）

1 Choose the correct answer.

(1) People say that Tokyo is a (future / futuristic) city.

(2) He is a (specialist / special person) in ecology.

(3) It seems to be really cold in (Antarctica / Africa).

(4) This native species (grows / grow) well in a mild climate.

2 Fill in the blanks to complete the sentences.

(1) 熱帯ではカラフルな魚をたくさん見ることができます。

You can see a lot of colorful fish in (　　　　) (　　　　).

(2) 私の父は地中海料理をよく作っていました。

My father used to cook (　　　　) food.

(3) この植物は温室で育てられました。

This plant was grown in a (　　　　).

(4) 彼女の家族はオリーブを庭で育てています。

Her family grows (　　　　) in their garden.

3 Reorder the words in brackets so that they can make sense.

(1) He is nice (me / for / everyone / except / to).

(2) They (into / their house / changed / a restaurant).

(3) Those Supertrees (to / meters / measure / tall / 50 / up).

(4) The plant (cold temperatures / requires / fruit / bear / to).

4 Translate the Japanese into English.

(1) その時，彼のシャツはずぶ濡れでした。

(2) その大学は埋立地に建てられました。

(3) あの建物の構造は水とエネルギーを節約します。

(4) この敷地を造園するのにいくらかかりますか？

1 Choose the correct answer.

(1) They were inspired by the (magical / magic) forest in *Princess Mononoke*.

(2) I could understand what that means (instantly / instant).

(3) Dancers use watches to (synthesize / synchronize) their movements.

(4) An example of (architect / architecture) is the Eiffel Tower in Paris.

2 Fill in the blanks to complete the sentences.

(1) 木の幹の主な機能は何ですか？

What is the main function of the (   ) of a tree?

(2) あのベンチはコンクリートで作られています。

That bench is made of (   ).

(3) 東京に住んでいるので，時々有名人を見かけます。

(   ) in Tokyo, I sometimes see famous people.

(4) 地元の食材を使って，特別食を彼らは提供しています。

They offer special meals, (   ) local ingredients.

3 Reorder the words in brackets so that they can make sense.

(1) Water (role / an / our body function / important / in / plays).

_____

(2) The author (from / some / cues / from / took / novels) the 1900s.

_____

(3) (Australia / giant / are / Karri trees / in / the) very tall.

_____

(4) The Supertrees (symbols / recognizable / Singapore / as / of / are).

_____

4 Translate the Japanese into English.

(1) 太陽光を集めるために，それは多くの枝を持っています。

_____

(2) その映画を観て，私は不思議な感覚になりました。

_____

(3) その機器は排気装置として機能します。

_____

(4) 母は音楽を聴きながら料理をします。（分詞構文を用いて）

_____

1　Choose the correct answer.

(1)　We need (glass / grass) panels for the windows.

(2)　The (steal / steel) grids supports the building.

(3)　The (arch / architecture) of my foot hurts.

(4)　Do not rely (in / on) your parents too much.

2　Fill in the blanks to complete the sentences.

(1)　ローマの建築の特徴は何ですか。

What are the features of (　　　　　) architecture?

(2)　石でできているので，あの椅子は座りづらいです。

(　　　　　) of stone, that chair is hard to sit on.

(3)　彼は私の理想の彼氏です。

He is my (　　　　　) boyfriend.

(4)　建物の中心に太い柱があります。

There is a thick (　　　　　) in the center of the building.

3　Reorder the words in brackets so that they can make sense.

(1)　Mica (used / has / products / for / electronic / been).

_____

(2)　Tiberius was the emperor, (world's / who / greenhouse / the / first / made).

_____

(3)　We can enjoy (time / way / this / lunch / in / our).

_____

(4)　The soccer player (legs / through / his / the ball / let).

_____

4　Translate the Japanese into English.

(1)　この塔の頂上からの光景は素晴らしいです。

_____

(2)　暑すぎたので，木の影に隠れました。

_____

(3)　2年前に建てられたので，その家は新しく見えます。（分詞構文を用いて）

_____

(4)　中国語で書かれていたので，その本は理解しづらかったです。（分詞構文を用いて）

_____

1 Choose the correct answer.

(1) Part of China in the south is in the (tropical / subtropical) region.

(2) (Typically / Professionally), we eat rice and miso soup in every meal.

(3) I have no (savings / saved) to buy it.

(4) She looks young, but (in / on) reality, she is over forty.

2 Fill in the blanks to complete the sentences.

(1) 有機野菜は体にいいですが，高価です。

(　　　　　　　) vegetables are good for you, but expensive.

(2) 霞がかっていたので，車は運転しませんでした。

It was (　　　　　　　), so I didn't drive.

(3) 紙上では，そのデザインは完璧に見えました。

(　　　　　　　) paper, the design looked perfect.

(4) 今日は湿度がとても高いです。

The (　　　　　　　) is really high today.

3 Reorder the words in brackets so that they can make sense.

(1) (in / two years / having / Australia / for / lived), Hiro now speaks English well.

_____

(2) A lack of sleep (gain / in / a / result / weight / can).

_____

(3) The Gardens by the Bay is (of / amazing / life / plant / an / collection).

_____

(4) (gathered / over / those / from / they / all) the world.

_____

4 Translate the Japanese into English.

(1) 間近で野生動物を見ることができました。

_____

(2) 省エネ技術についてもっと知りたいです。

_____

(3) 彼の仕事は壊れた排水管を修理することです。

_____

(4) 全てのことを考慮すれば，彼女が間違っているとは言えません。（分詞構文を用いて）

_____

1 Follow the instructions and rewrite the following sentences.

(1) <u>Since she knew well how to deal with emergencies,</u> she gave us instructions.

（下線部を分詞構文に）

_____ she gave us instructions.

(2) <u>Seen from the roof of the hotel,</u> this lake is beautiful. （下線部を接続詞を使った文に）

_____ this lake is beautiful.

(3) She introduced herself briefly <u>and began a speech.</u> （下線部を分詞構文に）

_____

(4) <u>Though she doesn't study so hard,</u> she will pass the entrance exam.

（下線部を分詞構文に）

_____ she will pass the entrance exam.

(5) <u>Climbing to the top of the mountain,</u> we can enjoy the great landscape.

（下線部を接続詞を使った文に）

_____ we can enjoy the great landscape.

(6) <u>Because I had already finished my homework,</u> I played a video game.

（下線部を分詞構文に）

_____ I played a video game.

(7) Don't use your mobile phone, <u>driving your car.</u> （下線部を接続詞を使った文に）

_____

(8) <u>Since I didn't have breakfast,</u> I'm starving now. （下線部を分詞構文に）

_____ I'm starving now.

(9) Opening the bottle, he poured the orange juice into my glass. （分詞構文ではない文に）

He _____

(10) <u>Since it is surrounded by flowers,</u> the park looks so beautiful. （下線部を分詞構文に）

_____ the park looks so beautiful.

(11) <u>Having failed several times,</u> he found out the cause. （下線部を接続詞を使った文に）

_____ he found out the cause.

2 Fill in the blanks to complete the sentences.

(1) 彼女は私の名前を呼びながら，私に駆け寄りました。

She ran to me, (　　　　　) (　　　　　) (　　　　　).

(2) 風邪を引いていたので，私は出かけるのを諦めました。

(　　　　　) a cold, I gave up going out.

(3) 今日，忙しくないなら，私といっしょに映画を見に行ってくれますか。

(　　　　) (　　　　) (　　　　　) today, could you go see a movie with me?

(4) 厳密に言えば，彼が言ったことは間違いです。

(　　　　) (　　　　　　), what he said is wrong.

(5) すべてを考慮すると，それは値段の価値があります。

(　　　　) (　　　　　) (　　　　　　), it's worth the price.

3 Reorder the words in brackets so that they can make sense.

(1) (on the phone / noticed / , / talking with / I / my friend) he was depressed.

_____

(2) (was / in his childhood / he / tough and bright / , / poor).

_____

(3) (to him / thanking him / , / I / his help / for / bowed).

_____

(4) (to / for him / can / attend / you / , / the meeting / asked) accept the request?

_____ accept the request?

(5) (, / we / admitting / cooperate / cannot / your proposal) with you.

_____

(6) (France / in French / she / , / having / is / never / proficient / been to).

_____

4 Translate the Japanese into English.

(1) いつも約束を守るので，彼は信頼できます。(分詞構文で)

He can be relied on, _____ .

(2) 気分が優れなかったので，彼女は学校を休んでいました。(分詞構文で)

_____ she was absent from school.

(3) 何度も会ったことがありましたが，私は彼女の名前が思い出せませんでした。(分詞構文で)

_____ I could not recall her name.

(4) 私の経験から判断すると，彼女はチームを率いるのには若すぎます。(分詞構文で)

_____ she is too young to lead the team.

(5) 天気が良ければ，私たちは明日，サイクリングに出かけます。(分詞構文で)

_____ we'll go cycling tomorrow.

Flying on the Longest Non-stop Flight in the World!

A few years ago, I got an email from my friend from college. She had moved to Singapore after graduation for work, but we still ①kept in touch. The email was an invitation to her wedding! She had met someone there and they were planning a wedding at one of Singapore's luxury hotels at the end of the year. What exciting news! I immediately

5　emailed her back telling her I would be there for her big day.

②It was only then that I thought "How does one get to Singapore?" I was living in New York City then, so I did a search on the Internet to find out about available flights. To my surprise, ③the flight times were so long—19 hours! I booked a flight on Singapore Airlines from Newark Liberty Airport in New Jersey, which is near New York City. I

10　later found out that the flight was the longest non-stop flight in the world at the time and covered about 10,000 miles.

Luckily, I could use my mileage to upgrade my ticket to business class. Spending 19 hours in economy did not sound very ④appealing at all! I felt both excited and nervous about spending such a long time in an airplane. I learned that the route was first flown

15　in 2013, but that it had been cancelled due to high fuel prices a few years later. By the time I flew, the price of fuel had fallen, and new technology and lightweight materials used to build airplanes allowed the airline to fly the route again.

Finally, my departure day came, and I headed to the airport to check in. On board, I was surprised at the variety of food available. I spoke to one of the flight attendants and

20　she told me that there was an in-flight chef and that a total of 480 menu combinations were possible during the flight.

The business class seat was comfortable and equipped with a state-of-the-art entertainment system with 1200 hours of content. There was a pull-out desk that fit my laptop and the wide seat could be converted into a flat bed. I could sleep a little, in fact,

25　and when I arrived at Singapore's Changi Airport after 19 hours, I felt refreshed.

I had a great time at my friend's wedding, but ⑤my experience on the longest flight in the world was also unforgettable. Singapore was an interesting city to visit, and I hope to be back again someday!

(412 words)

注：mileage　マイレージサービス（旅客の搭乗距離に応じてポイントがつくサービス）

66

(1) 下線部①および④の意味に最も近い語句を選び，それぞれ記号で答えなさい。

    ① ア missed each other   イ kept away from each other

        ウ kept each other in mind   エ contacted each other

    ④ ア disappointing   イ attractive

        ウ expensive   エ surprising

                                          ①(   ) ④(   )

(2) 下線部②を日本語に直した次の文の（   ）を補い，文を完成させなさい。ただし，then の内容を具体的に述べること。

    私は（   ），「どうやってシンガポールに行くのだろう」と考えた。

(3) 下線部③が可能となった理由を示すように（   ）に日本語を補いなさい。

    飛行機製造のための（   ）と

    （   ）が使われたから。

(4) 本文の内容で下線部⑤に当てはまらないものを1つ選び，記号で答えなさい。

    ア The passengers had the food on the plane which had been cooked beforehand.

    イ The passenger on the flight could enjoy many kinds of food.

    ウ Some seats on the plane were suitable for working with a PC.

    エ Some seats on the plane were designed so that the passengers would not get tired after the long flight.

                                                             (   )

(5) 本文の内容と一致するものを1つ選び，記号で答えなさい。

    ア Passengers had to visit the airport to get information about flight tickets.

    イ The airplane the author took stopped at an airport on the way to Singapore.

    ウ The author could obtain a ticket for the higher class of the flight.

    エ The change to another type of fuel used for airplanes enabled the flight to fly for many hours.

                                                             (   )

1 Choose the correct answer.

(1) (Dr. / Mrs.) Tanaka is a university lecturer. He teaches biology.

(2) The (production / produce) of the cars have been stopped at Toyota for a week.

(3) The army used satellite (image / imagery) to make the map.

(4) I saw a (space craft / spacecraft) coming back to Earth.

2 Fill in the blanks to complete the sentences.

(1) 大学での専攻は天体物理学でした。

My major was (   ) at college.

(2) 神は存在すると信じています。

I believe that God (   ).

(3) 私の父は作曲家です。

My father is a (   ).

(4) 昨晩私たちは帝国ホテルに泊まりました。

We stayed at the (   ) Hotel.

3 Reorder the words in brackets so that they can make sense.

(1) Abeno Harukas is (other / than / building / any / taller) in Osaka.

_____

(2) He is (who / NASA / joined / astrophysicist / has / an).

_____

(3) Pluto is (a planet / longer / as / no / considered).

_____

(4) Hokkaido is (other / any / distant / than / more / from here) prefecture.

_____

4 Translate the Japanese into English.

(1) あそこから地平線を見ることができます。

_____

(2) 彼らは彼以外の者全員に事実を明らかにしました。

_____

(3) この論文を書くのは大変でした。

_____

(4) このようにして，彼女は博士課程の学生になりました。

_____

1 Choose the correct answer.

(1) We would like to visit many tourist (attracts / attractions) in Paris.

(2) I like the (thrill / thrilling) of driving fast.

(3) The city was named in honor (to / of) the city's founder.

(4) The (portrait / landscape) of Brian May was drawn by a famous artist.

2 Fill in the blanks to complete the sentences.

(1) 冥王星の探索は最近始まりました。

The (   ) of Pluto began recently.

(2) 宇宙船の接近を見に出かけました。

I went out to see the (   ) of a spacecraft.

(3) 8月中旬に京都へ行きます。

We are going to Kyoto in (   ).

(4) "mouse" と "house" は韻を踏みます。

Mouse is a (   ) for "house".

3 Reorder the words in brackets so that they can make sense.

(1) I want (together / to / the two images / you / put).

_____

(2) They (a song / celebrate / friends' / released / their / to) marriage.

_____

(3) The author (be / on / invited / to / present / was) the opening night.

_____

(4) Alan Stern realized (the / inspiring / was / project / whole / how).

_____

4 Translate the Japanese into English.

(1) 彼を頼れるかどうか疑問に思っていました。

_____

(2) どんな場合でも，彼女は一生懸命働きます。

_____

(3) スマートフォンでステレオ写真を撮ることができます。

_____

(4) この映画の方が昨日観たものよりも面白くなさそうです。

_____

1 Choose the correct answer.

(1) Let's get (down / up) to business.

(2) The plane is about to (taking / take) off.

(3) The police officer put me (in / on) hold.

(4) (As / So) he told you, his thesis became famous.

2 Fill in the blanks to complete the sentences.

(1) これを明日提出しなければなりません。

I have to (　　　　　　) this to my boss tomorrow.

(2) 彼女は自分の間違いを認めました。

She (　　　　　　) that she was wrong.

(3) あなたの子どもがもし物理が苦手ならどうしますか。

What if your kids are bad at (　　　　　　)?

(4) 彼が言ったことを文字通りに受け取らない方がよいです。

You should not take what he said (　　　　　　).

3 Reorder the words in brackets so that they can make sense.

(1) You need to clean (the / in / your room / place / up / first).

_____

(2) People (unique / what / often / makes / wonder / us).

_____

(3) Her new (to / her / brought / TV / song / back).

_____

(4) His band's success (he / shown / has / is / that / clearly) good at music.

_____

4 Translate the Japanese into English.

(1) 明日までに博士論文を書き終えたいです。

_____

(2) 私たちは宿題にすぐ取りかかるべきです。

_____

(3) 太陽系について教えてください。

_____

(4) 明日テストがあるかどうか知っていますか。

_____

1　Choose the correct answer.

(1)　We don't want to (interact / interest) with strangers much.

(2)　The band has just finished their new (recordings / records).

(3)　If I (were / had been) a bird, I would enjoy flying in the sky.

(4)　If I (knew / had known) that I was sick, I wouldn't have gone to the event.

2　Fill in the blanks to complete the sentences.

(1)　これは国の遺産です。

This is a (　　　　　　) of the country.

(2)　様々な墓石がここにはあります。

There are a variety of (　　　　　　) here.

(3)　留学すれば，多くのカルチャーショックに出くわすでしょう。

If you study abroad, you will (　　　　　) (　　　　　) a lot of culture shock.

(4)　もし彼がもっと注意深かったなら，交通事故を避けられただろうに。

If he had been more careful, he (　　　　) (　　　　) (　　　　　　) the car accident.

3　Reorder the words in brackets so that they can make sense.

(1)　John Lennon (woman / married / Japanese / was / to / a).

_____

(2)　Those people are at (top / very / the / of / game / their).

_____

(3)　(the / watching / flyby / spacecraft / the / of) was so exciting.

_____

(4)　The victory (were / out / celebrations / to / beamed / the world).

_____

4　Translate the Japanese into English.

(1)　私たちは元日に祖父母の家に行きます。

_____

(2)　それは地球から 40 億マイルも離れたところを旅していました。

_____

(3)　もし昨晩暇だったら，君と出かけていたのに。

_____

(4)　世間の注目は地球に帰ってきたボイジャー 2 号に集まっていました。

_____

1 Follow the instructions and rewrite the following sentences.

(1) Tokyo is the most crowded city in Japan.   （比較級を使って同じ意味の文に）

_____

(2) Mr. Nakamura plays the most important role in saving lives.

（比較級を使って同じ意味の文に）

_____

(3) The weather wasn't good, so the event wasn't successful.   （仮定法過去完了の文に）

_____

(4) You were with me, so I could put up with the anxiety.   （仮定法過去完了の文に）

_____

(5) She wasn't angry, so I didn't go to see her in person.   （仮定法過去完了の文に）

_____

2 Fill in the blanks to complete the sentences.

(1) 私たちにとって時間ほど貴重なものはありません。

(   ) is (   ) precious than time for us.

(2) あなたはこの挑戦が失敗に終わるかどうかを気にする必要はありません。

You don't have to (   ) (   ) this challenge will end up in failure.

(3) あなたがこの地図を送らなかったら，私たちは時間に間に合ってそこに着けませんでした。

If you (   ) (   ) (   ) this map, we (   ) (   )
(   ) there in time.

(4) あなたは会議が中止になったことを言うべきだったのに。

You (   ) (   ) (   ) me that the meeting had been canceled.

(5) 苦情の処理において，彼女よりスキルがあるスタッフは他にいません。

(   ) (   ) staff member has (   ) skills than her in dealing
with complaints.

(6) 私は別の方法を選ぶべきかどうか考えています。

I'm (   ) (   ) I should choose another way.

(7) 私たちがその誤解に気づかなかったら，何が起こったでしょうか。

What (   ) (   ) (   ) if we (   ) (   )
(   ) the misunderstanding?

(8) この試験は他のどの試験よりも英語の能力を評価することができます。

This test can assess our English ability (   ) (   ) (   )
(   ) (   ).

3 Reorder the words in brackets so that they can make sense.

(1) If you (have / we / explained / less time / , / taken / had / might / the rule) to understand it.

_____

(2) (than / more / nothing / gargling / is / effective) for preventing a cold.

_____

(3) (will / you / whether / right or wrong / tell / time / are).

_____

(4) If (been / had / his fine play / there / not), (would / lost / have / the game / our team).

_____

(5) (he / sure / I'm / said / a thing / if / not / such) in earnest.

_____

(6) Mr. Nishida (than / has / member / longer / any / performed / other) in the orchestra.

_____

(7) I (for her / she / have / if / the client / asked / met / had / could / me).

_____

(8) (than / other / is / no / company / more famous) ABC Ad in advertising.

_____

(9) (is / judge / the person / would / appropriate / whether / you) for the position?

_____

4 Translate the Japanese into English.

(1) もしあなたが私の電話番号を知っていたら，私にもっと早く電話で連絡できましたか。

_____

(2) 私は専門家にその実験が成功であったかどうかを聞きたいです。(実験 = experiment)

_____

(3) 私たちは道を間違えています。角で左に曲がるべきではありませんでした。
We are on the wrong street. _____

(4) あなたが私たちの会社への入社に興味があるかどうか知らせてください。
Let _____ .

(5) 彼は先生の助言に従っていれば，その試験に合格したでしょう。

_____

(6) このタイプは他のどの携帯電話よりも多機能です。
This type _____ .

(7) そんなに奇妙なことが本当に起こるのかどうか疑問に思います。

（～を疑問に思う = doubt，奇妙な = strange）

_____

A Museum Dedicated to Rock and Roll Music

The Rock and Roll Hall of Fame and Museum in Cleveland, Ohio celebrates the history of rock music and honors the contributions of ①(   ) who played important roles in the genre's development over the years. Several cities were considered for the location of the museum, but in the end, ②it was Cleveland that won. Many believe that
5 the reason was because a radio disc jockey named Alan Freed had first used the term "rock and roll" in the 1950s there.

When visiting the museum, you'll find an array of ③artifacts displayed like any other museum, such as instruments used by famous musicians, stage costumes, pages with song lyrics written on them, original album art, posters, and photos. The museum also
10 has an extensive research library.

To get into the Rock and Roll Hall of Fame, 25 years must have passed since an artist's first recording. Each year's nominees are selected by a committee of rock historians. Subsequently, an international group of around 500 rock experts vote on them and those receiving the highest number of votes are inducted into the Hall of Fame.
15 Each year, between five and seven musicians are given the honor. An official ceremony and concert are held in New York City each year to honor the new members with many of the inductees themselves performing live.

As of 2021, 338 artists had been admitted into the Hall of Fame. Among the first group in 1986 were superstars like Elvis Presley and Ray Charles. The first female artist
20 was admitted a year later with the addition of Aretha Franklin. Other notable inductees included Michael Jackson in 2001 and Whitney Houston in 2020.

Though the history of rock music is short, the Rock and Roll Hall of Fame and Museum serves as a place for everyone to remember ④(   ) musicians who have been so important to the music industry so far. Who do you think will be admitted into the
25 Hall of Fame among your current favorite musicians? ⑤It's really anyone's guess.

(334 words)

注：The Rock and Roll Hall of Fame (and Museum)　ロックの殿堂(博物館)

(1) 下線部①および④の（　　　　）に入る同じ１語を答えなさい。

_____

(2) 下線部②の理由を日本語で説明しなさい。

_____

_____

(3) 下線部③の例として正しくないものを１つ選び，記号で答えなさい。

ア　tools used by musicians　　イ　clothes for performances

ウ　autographs　　　　　　　　エ　papers with words for songs

（　　　）

(4) ロックの殿堂のメンバーに選ばれる過程として正しくないものを１つ選び，記号で答えなさい。

ア　Persons that should be suggested for members are selected.

イ　Nominees of the Hall of Fame play in front of judges.

ウ　Each expert expresses her or his own opinion on who should be a new member.

エ　Nominees that are supported by the most experts become new members.

（　　　）

(5) 下線部⑤の意味に最も近いものを１つ選び，記号で答えなさい。

ア　No one knows the answer in advance.

イ　Anyone who is interested should give ideas.

ウ　We shouldn't speculate about something that we don't know.

（　　　）

(6) 本文の内容と一致するものを１つ選び，記号で答えなさい。

ア　Only one city was considered for the place of the museum from the beginning.

イ　We can study something concerning rock music in the museum.

ウ　Artists that just made their debut may be selected as a member of the Hall of Fame.

エ　Aretha Franklin was included in the first group of members of the Hall of Fame.

（　　　）

1   Choose the correct answer.

(1)   Black people have been treated (unfairly / fairly) in the United States.

(2)   (A / The) number of people eat bread every day in the world.

(3)   He is an (well-known / unknown) actor. Not many people know him.

(4)   Women's (equality / equal) has been a major topic these days.

2   Fill in the blanks to complete the sentences.

(1)   明らかに，あなたの方が私よりも遥かに勉強しています。

Obviously, you study (　　　　　　) more (　　　　　　) me.

(2)   この30年間で性別による役割は変化してきています。

(　　　　　　) roles have been changing in these three decades.

(3)   称賛されていない英雄が歴史上には多くいます。

There are a lot of (　　　　　　) heroes in history.

(4)   彼らのチームはついに目標を達成しました。

Their team has finally (　　　　　　) their goal.

3   Reorder the words in brackets so that they can make sense.

(1)   You (look / to / only / enough / closely / need).

_____

(2)   The gap between rich people (becoming / poor / and / wider / people / is).

_____

(3)   The Mediterranean diet (been / as / long / promoted / a / has) typical healthy diet.

_____

(4)   The report (40th / that / in / Japan / shows / came in) the 2021 global rankings.

_____

4   Translate the Japanese into English.

(1)   明日は全国的に雨が降るでしょう。

_____

(2)   今日，ますます多くの外国人が日本を訪れています。

_____

(3)   先生が昨日言ったことはとても印象的でした。

_____

(4)   彼女は44歳の小学校の先生です。

_____

1   Choose the correct answer.

(1)   We are going to dance at the school (fair / unfair).

(2)   I got (sponsorship / scholarship) to work in Canada.

(3)   My wife and I went to the (Philippine / Philippines) last month.

(4)   He was (distinguishing / distinguished) from the other boys.

2   Fill in the blanks to complete the sentences.

(1)   私の祖父は孤児院で育ったと聞きました。

     I heard that my grandfather grew up in an (　　　　　　　).

(2)   その国が発展するにはいくらかの経済的援助が必要です。

     The country needs some (　　　　　　　) aid to develop.

(3)   カンボジアは観光客にとても人気の場所です。

     (　　　　　　　) is a very popular place for tourists.

(4)   彼女の誕生日にアクセサリーをあげました。

     I gave my girlfriend an (　　　　　　　) for her birthday.

3   Reorder the words in brackets so that they can make sense.

(1)   (held / craft / will / fairs / be / some) here this summer.

     _____

(2)   She has lost (in / key chain / neighborhood / her / her).

     _____

(3)   I found a (in Germany / to / my visa / sponsor / stay / for).

     _____

(4)   They have been (their / a donor / for / for / looking / baby).

     _____

4   Translate the Japanese into English.

(1)   地元で育った野菜は安価です。

     _____

(2)   私たちは順番に赤ちゃんの世話をします。

     _____

(3)   私は英語を話せませんし，ましてやフランス語など話せません。

     _____

(4)   このウェブサイトは外国人向けに特別にデザインされました。

     _____

1 Choose the correct answer.

(1) (Further more / Furthermore), the organization helps orphanages nationwide.

(2) We were always (welcomed / welcoming) by those friends.

(3) Self-confidence and responsibility are (tangible / intangible).

(4) I have gained some experience (in / on) teaching.

2 Fill in the blanks to complete the sentences.

(1) 貧困は最も大きな社会問題の一つです。

(　　　　　　　) is one of the biggest social issues.

(2) 我々は次の世代を教育しなければなりません。

We must (　　　　　　) the next generation.

(3) 会社をよくするには，従業員はもっと協力しあった方がいいです。

To make the company better, workers should (　　　　　) (　　　　　) each other more.

(4) 私の友達は非営利団体に勤めています。

My friend works for a (　　　　　　) organization.

3 Reorder the words in brackets so that they can make sense.

(1) A large number of scholars (health / research / conduct / mental / on).

_____

(2) The government (less / people / support / privileged / must).

_____

(3) (expensive / joining / by / tours / these), I can finally prove myself rich.

_____

(4) People have been trying (of / raise / awareness / equality / to / gender).

_____

4 Translate the Japanese into English.

(1) 私の母は全く運転しません。

_____

(2) 彼のいとこはますます背が高くなっています。

_____

(3) そのケガをした男の人はほとんど歩けませんでした。

_____

(4) あの会社は日本の先生向けに教材を開発しています。

_____

1   Choose the correct answer.

(1) For me, (unhappiness / happiness) is achieving a number of goals.

(2) In his (freshman / freshmen) year in college, he got run over by a car.

(3) I have (overcome / overcame) a lot of changes throughout my life.

(4) How can we help (underprivileged / privileged) children?

2   Fill in the blanks to complete the sentences.

(1) 私たちは最近離婚しました。

We got (   ) recently.

(2) 幸運なことに私はその事故に巻き込まれませんでした。

It was (   ) that I did not get involved in the accident.

(3) 心理的ストレスは体にも影響します。

(   ) stress affects our body.

(4) 犯人はまだ特定されていません。

The criminal has not been (   ) yet.

3   Reorder the words in brackets so that they can make sense.

(1) Their (end / failed / the / attempt / in).

_____

(2) (the / gone / that / storm / now / is), we can finally go out.

_____

(3) We haven't (each / for / a / other / seen / while).

_____

(4) Mary's (to / effort / turned / a great / be / out) success.

_____

4   Translate the Japanese into English.

(1) あなたの声はほとんど聞こえませんでした。

_____

(2) 誰が正しいか証明してください。

_____

(3) 父に結婚はいいものかどうか尋ねました。

_____

(4) トムはめったにお酒を飲みません。

_____

1 Fill in the blanks to complete the sentences.

(1) 彼は自信をつけるにつれ，態度がますます積極的になりました。

As he had more confidence, his attitude got (　　　　　) and (　　　　　) positive.

(2) 私たちはその理論をほとんど理解できません。

We (　　　　　) (　　　　　) understand the theory.

(3) その野菜の価格は1年中めったに変動しません。

The price of the vegetable (　　　　　) (　　　　　) throughout the year.

(4) 彼はあまり活動的ではなく，海外に行ったことがありません。

He is not very active, and he (　　　　) (　　　　) (　　　　) abroad.

(5) 私たちは卒業してからますますお互いに連絡を取らなくなりました。

We have contacted each other (　　　　) (　　　　) (　　　　) often since we graduated.

(6) その英語表現は実際にはめったに使われません。

The English expression (　　　　) (　　　　) (　　　　) in practice.

(7) 私は子どもたちが私からますます遠くに離れていく気がします。

I feel that my children are moving (　　　　) (　　　　) (　　　　) away from me.

(8) 子どもたちに知らない人に決してついて行かないように言ってください。

Tell the children (　　　　) (　　　　) follow strangers.

(9) チームがプロジェクトを進めるにつれ，事態はますます悪くなりました。

Things went (　　　　) (　　　　) (　　　　) as the team advanced the project.

2 Reorder the words in brackets so that they can make sense.

(1) The development of technology (to / it / get information / easier and easier / makes).

_____

(2) (are / without PCs / scarcely / there / companies) at present.

_____

(3) (unless / betray / lose trust / you / never / want to / others).

_____

(4) We (remember / grow / each time / angrier and angrier / the fact / we).

_____

(5) She (hardly / so bright / she / is / the same mistake / that / makes) twice.

_____

(6) (darker and darker / the storm / turned / because of / the sky).

_____

(7) Fortunately, (affected / was / the heavy rain / the area / by / scarcely).

_____

(8) (becoming / for / is / bilingual people / greater and greater / the need)?

_____

(9) (are / one member / rarely / by / important matters / determined).

_____

(10) I (promoted to / that / I / dreamed / would be / never) manager.

_____

(11) The things (complain about / seldom / are / customers / improved).

_____

(12) He (speaks to / and / is / scarcely / anyone / quiet).

_____

(13) (seldom / that / is / Westerners / true / take a bath / it)?

_____

3 Translate the Japanese into English.

(1) 彼女は語彙を増やすことにますます熱心になってきました。

She has _____ .

(2) 私は彼が退職する時に残したメッセージを決して忘れません。

_____ he left when he retired.

(3) 生徒が教科に興味を持てば，ますます得意になるでしょう。

If students become interested in a subject, _____ .

(4) 彼女はトッププレイヤーのグループに仲間入りしてから，ますます懸命に練習しました。

_____ after she joined the top group of players.

(5) 彼女は必ず私たちの期待を上回ります。(never を使って，期待 = expectation)

_____

(6) 私の父は週末，ほとんど家にいません。

_____

(7) 私は虫歯がたくさんあってもめったに歯医者にはいきません。

_____ no matter how many bad teeth I have.

(8) 私たちは素晴らしい音楽を聴いて飽きることは決してないです。

_____

(9) 私はコンサートが始まるのを待てません。(hardly を使って)

_____

(10) 新たなことに挑戦することを決して恐れてはなりません。(be afraid of ～を使って)

_____

Women's Role in Politics

In 2015, 193 countries adopted the 17 Sustainable Development Goals (SDGs) promising to achieve them by 2030. The fifth SDG is to "achieve gender equality and empower all women and girls." To work towards ①this goal, increasing the role of women in politics is essential. Let's examine the current situation in politics regarding women's
5 participation around the world.

As of 2021, women were heads of state in only 22 countries worldwide and 119 countries had never had a woman serve as a leader, including Japan. More female leaders like New Zealand's Jacinda Ardern are important role models for young women today.

As for government ministers, women represent only 21 percent of them worldwide.
10 Only 14 countries have achieved ②gender parity, meaning that women represent at least 50 percent of ministerial positions. In Japan, under Prime Minister Suga, there were only two women chosen to serve on his cabinet, down from three in Abe's previous administration.

In national parliaments, only 25 percent are women and only four countries have achieved a rate of 50 percent. The African country of Rwanda leads the world with 61
15 percent, while both Cuba and Bolivia are at 53 percent. A total of 19 countries have reached at least 40 percent and those include nine countries in Europe, five in Latin America and the Caribbean, four in Africa, and one in the Pacific.

One of the policies that many countries with higher female political representation have implemented is ③gender quotas. The policy makes laws that either mandate the number
20 of female candidates required to run in elections or reserve a certain number of seats for women in political bodies.

There is evidence that ④more female involvement in politics is beneficial in terms of policy. For example, research on local councils in India showed that the number of drinking water projects in areas with women-led councils was 62 percent higher than those with
25 men-led councils. In Norway, researchers found that the presence of women on city councils had a direct relationship to more childcare availability.

It's clear that much progress still must be made to achieve the goal stated in the fifth SDG. But hopefully, the success of some countries regarding female political participation will help more countries move faster towards the goal. This will certainly benefit not
30 only women, but all of society.   (387 words)

注：Sustainable Development Goals (SDGs)　持続可能な開発目標

(1) 下線部①を具体的に説明するため，（　　　）を補いなさい。

（
　　）

という目標

(2) 下線部②について，ここではどういうことかを日本語で説明しなさい。

_____

(3) 下線部③を具体的に表す英文として正しいものを1つ選び，記号で答えなさい。

ア　the percentage of women's votes in elections

イ　the percentage of the support from women that political bodies receive

ウ　the number of political representatives receiving the most female votes

エ　the number of female political representatives in groups

（　　　）

(4) 下線部④の例を2つ日本語で説明しなさい。

1つ目：_____

_____

2つ目：_____

_____

(5) 本文の内容と一致するものを1つ選び，記号で答えなさい。

ア　A female leader had never emerged in more than 100 countries when this article was written.

イ　The rate of female ministers was remarkably high under Suga's administration.

ウ　There are 19 countries in whose parliaments women are at least 40%, including Japan.

エ　The success of female political participation will have no influence on an entire society.

（　　　）

Useful Phrases & Idioms

I got this job after *a series of* tests.
At the beginning of the party, the student made a short speech.
You *ought to do* some exercise every day.

I *wrote down* the title of the book.
Let's *proceed to discuss* the next topic.
Hiroshi stayed at home *instead of* his little brother.
In fact, I was in the library when Tom visited me.

Mind you, keep it secret.

Even if you don't understand the language, you can enjoy this movie.
I won't *back down* until you accept my request.
Finally Mr. Oka *gave in* and bought the toy for his son.
From *my point of view*, you are wrong.
Tom speaks Chinese *as well as* English.
At a glance, I found the woman was scared.

I *used to swim* in this river in my childhood.
To start with, thank you for inviting me to the party.
Where *on earth* did Mike go?
What do you want a new smartphone *for*?
Koalas *live* only *on* plants.
We still have *plenty of* food in our house.

The cat and the dog *cuddle up with* each other.
For one thing, Jill studies hard.

"Will you forgive me?" "*It depends.*"
I sleep seven hours a day *on average*.
I want to sleep for *at least* seven hours.
I spoke in a louder voice to *get everyone's attention*.
We should protect wild animals, *for instance*, tigers.
"Are there aliens in the universe?" "*Who knows?*"
Let's *put* this matter *aside* for a while.

Lesson 2 Part 4
- [ ] allow ~ to *do*

This machine *allows you to cut* wood in any shapes.

Lesson 3 Part 1
- [ ] deal with ~
- [ ] spend *one's* life
- [ ] warn ~ away from ...

Every country has to *deal with* problems of global warming.
Mary *spent* all *her life* as a great singer.
The police are *warning* people *away from* the scene of the accident.

Lesson 3 Part 2
- [ ] keep ~ away from ...

Keep yourself *away from* the fire.

Lesson 3 Part 3
- [ ] in a moment
- [ ] care for ~
- [ ] stand off

Hiroshi will come *in a moment.*
Mr. Oka *cares for* three kids.
The coaches had to *stand off* the line during the football game.

Lesson 3 Part 4
- [ ] have ~ on *one's* own
- [ ] one by one
- [ ] rather than ~
- [ ] turn ~ into ...

I want to *have* a room *on my own.*
The teacher is calling her students' names *one by one.*
I want to go out today *rather than* read the book.
Heat *turns* ice *into* water.

Lesson 4 Part 1
- [ ] in addition to ~
- [ ] make a difference
- [ ] begin to *do*
- [ ] prepare for ~

In addition to food, she gave the poor boy some money.
Her effort *made a* big *difference* in her own life.
The ship *began to move* slowly.
Students enjoy *preparing for* the school festival.

Lesson 4 Part 2
- [ ] quite a few ~

There are *quite a few* students from foreign countries in our school.

Lesson 4 Part 3
- [ ] aim to *do*
- [ ] provide ~ with ...
- [ ] make use of ~
- [ ] up to ~

I *aim to improve* my speaking ability.
My father works very hard to *provide* me *with* quality education.
Journalists write articles by *making use of* much data.
The price of the painting rose *up to* 100 million dollars.

Lesson 4 Part 4
- [ ] have ~ in common
- [ ] other than ~
- [ ] regard ~ as ...
- [ ] in order to *do*

We *have* many things *in common*, such as hobby and fashion.
I would like a dish *other than* pizza because I ate it yesterday.
Takeshi is *regarded as* the best soccer player in this school.
I must study harder *in order to pass* the exam.

Useful Phrases & Idioms

Lesson 5 Part 1
- [ ] put on ~
- [ ] a large number of ~

Some students are going to *put on* a play at the school festival.
I am going to make a speech in front of *a large number of* people.

Lesson 5 Part 2
- [ ] ~ as well

Jim plays the piano, and the guitar *as well*.

Lesson 5 Part 3
- [ ] a variety of ~
- [ ] engage in ~
- [ ] attempt to *do*

You can choose a T-shirt from *a variety of* colors.
My father was *engaged in* making TV programs.
Takashi did not *attempt to go* out in the rain yesterday.

Lesson 5 Part 4
- [ ] look back on ~

Every weekend, my father *looks back on* his high school days.

Lesson 6 Part 1
- [ ] be busy *doing*
- [ ] participate in ~
- [ ] by *oneself*
- [ ] as in ~
- [ ] those who ~
- [ ] what's more

Takashi *is busy practicing* for the next basketball game.
More than 100 students *participated in* the meeting.
The door opens *by itself*.
In Tokyo, *as in* most big cities, you can find a lot of libraries.
There are *those who* can speak more than three languages.
Ken plays the guitar. *What's more*, he sings very well too.

Lesson 6 Part 2
- [ ] make a decision
- [ ] What if ~ ?

My brother needs more time before he can *make a decision*.
What if the bus is late?

Lesson 6 Part 3
- [ ] run over

My sister is always careful because she does not want to be *run over* by a car.

Lesson 7 Part 1
- [ ] be made up of ~
- [ ] bit by bit
- [ ] not ~ either ...

The reading club is *made up of* fifteen people.
To make good soup, you should add milk *bit by bit*.
I *cannot* accept *either* of the two plans.

Lesson 7 Part 2
- [ ] by nature

Amy is a quiet girl *by nature*.

Lesson 7 Part 3
- [ ] name ~ after ...
- [ ] contribute to ~
- [ ] join up
- [ ] object to ~

My father *named* me *after* a famous baseball player.
Her father *contributed to* the newspaper.
Five students *joined up* in the volunteer group.
I *object to* the new plan.

Lesson 8 Part 1
- ☐ change 〜 to[into] ...
- ☐ except for 〜

My father asked me to *change* a bad habit *to* a good habit.
The shop is open every day *except for* the first Monday of the month.

Lesson 8 Part 2
- ☐ take a cue from 〜
- ☐ play an important role in 〜

If you don't know what to do, *take a cue from* others' experience.
Robots will *play an important role in* care business.

Lesson 8 Part 3
- ☐ rely on 〜
- ☐ let 〜 through ...
- ☐ in this way

Hiroki *relies on* his parents' support.
The baseball player *let* the ball *through* the legs.
In this way, Ken made his dream come true.

Lesson 8 Part 4
- ☐ result in 〜
- ☐ up close

The driver's lack of sleep *resulted in* the accident.
Take a look at this rare flower *up close*.

Lesson 9 Part 2
- ☐ in honor of 〜

The party was held *in honor of* the winner of the Nobel Prize.

Lesson 9 Part 3
- ☐ in the first place
- ☐ be about to *do*
- ☐ work on
- ☐ on hold
- ☐ get down to 〜

I need to clean up my room *in the first place*.
The concert *is about to begin*.
Tom *works on* his presentation for next Monday.
The construction of the bridge is *on hold* now.
We can *get down to* our work if these problems are cleared.

Lesson 9 Part 4
- ☐ come across 〜

I *came across* my old friend in the airport yesterday.

Lesson 10 Part 1
- ☐ a number of 〜

We need *a number of* volunteers to clean the park.

Lesson 10 Part 2
- ☐ much less 〜
- ☐ in turn

John cannot write *hiragana*, *much less kanji*.
I am going to read ten books *in turn* this weekend.

Lesson 10 Part 4
- ☐ now that 〜
- ☐ for a while
- ☐ to this day
- ☐ turn out to be 〜
- ☐ in the end

Now that the rain has stopped, let's go!
Please wait here *for a while*.
Even *to this day*, I clearly remember my promise with Kana.
What the boy had told us *turned out to be* true.
Their challenge failed *in the end*.

Ambition
English Communication I
Workbook

編集　開隆堂編集部
発行　開隆堂出版株式会社
　　　代表者　岩塚太郎
　　　〒113-8608　東京都文京区向丘1-13-1
　　　電話03-5684-6115（編集）
　　　https://www.kairyudo.co.jp/
印刷　株式会社大熊整美堂
販売　開隆館出版販売株式会社
　　　〒113-8608　東京都文京区向丘1-13-1
　　　電話03-5684-6118（販売）

■表紙デザイン
畑中 猛